ICE HOCKE, (1930)
by Major BM Patton

A facsimile reprint of the original 1936 edition with
new introduction, author biography and appendices

Interesting Books...
...Fascinating Subjects!

POSH UP NORTH
Publishing
www.poshupnorth.com

Originally published in 1936 by Routledge
This edition published in Great Britain in October 2020 by
Posh Up North Publishing,
Beckenham Road, Wallasey

ISBN-13: 978-1-909643-39-0

Original edition © 1936
Major Bethune Minet Patton (1876-1939)

LIST OF ILLUSTRATIONS

Between Centre Pages 83 and 84

Notes for 2020 Reprint Edition:

The illustrations in the original 1936 edition were inserted on glossy inlays between numbered pages. In order to keep the correct page numbers for the written text, we have placed the photos together in the middle of the book and re-ordered them to make better chronological sense.

Photos marked * were not included in the original 1936 edition.

LIST OF CONTENTS
2020 Reprint Edition

INTRODUCTION

Much of the information contained in this book has been quoted, recycled, referred to and repeated in practically every other book that has ever covered the fascinating history of ice hockey in Britain - and with very good reason.

The original author - Peter Patton - was there right at the start and subsequently involved in all the major developments of the game in this country, taking it from a quaint form of bandy played outdoors on frozen ponds to a proper indoor sport with recognised rules, teams and equipment.

"Ice Hockey" was published in 1936 - the year that the Great Britain team won the Olympic gold medal for the one and only time - and has never been reprinted. Patton died in 1939 and when ice hockey resumed after World War 2, the game had already changed a great deal from the game that it had been prior to the war, and immeasurably from the embryonic version of the sport that Patton had toured Europe with in the early years of the century.

With continuing developments over the years - rule changes, safety measures, inprovements in equipment, better facilities - and globalisation expanding opportunities ever further, ice hockey in the 21st century is now even more far removed from the game that Patton first played, but that doesn't make his words and reminiscences any less relevant.

In fact, as we move ever further away in time from these early steps, it makes it an ideal time to to revisit those days and read for oursleves in his own words what the man who was in the thick of it all had to say about it.

With the benefits and facilities of modern technology, and in a move that we hope that Patton himself would have heartily approved of, we have decided to make his book – which has been practically impossible to get hold of for over 70 years without shelling out a small fortune to a rare book dealer - available to everybody at a reasonable selling price and we hope that you enjoy reading it.

*Ice Sports - Then. A view of the old Prince's Ice Skating Rink that Patton would
have been familiar with – staging a curling match in 1910 (Photo courtesy
David Smith - Scottish Curler, May 2008 and www.curlinghistory.blogspot.com)*

*Ice Sports – Now: A scene Patton would probably not have recognised – Widnes
wild women's team player Emma Pearson (#33) making an appearance for the
men's team in a league game against Blackburn in 2019
(Photo by Hannah Walker / Widnes Wild Ice Hockey Club)*

Major Bethune Minet Patton, RASC (Ret'd) – A BRIEF BIOGRAPHY

Bethune Minet "Peter" Patton (5th March 1876 - 10th April 1939) was an ice hockey player and administrator.

He is credited with bringing ice hockey to Britain and helping to spread the sport to Europe.

General Biography

Bethune Minet Patton – or "Peter" as he preferred to be called - was born on 5th March 1876 in London into a highly prestigious military family. His parents were Henry Bethune Patton (1835-1915) CB, VD and his second wife Georgina Emma Minet (1845-1918).

His first name "Bethune" came from a several times "great" grand mother Mary Bethune, who had married an earlier Patton in 1749 and who came from a highly regarded ancient Scottish family.

Many descendents from that branch used the name Bethune so that the family connection would continue. The names of Bethune and Patton feature prominently across the British military during the 19th century.

The name "Minet" was his mother's maiden name. Georgina Emma Minet was the second youngest of 6 daughters born to Charles and Leah Minet. Emma's family were in Dresden at the time of her birth and she was registered by the British Chaplaincy there.

BM Patton's father was a particularly impressive figure. He was a local magistrate and Deputy Lieutenant of Shropshire.

A former Captain with the 27th Inniskillings and the Bengal Horse Artillery, he was decorated for his services during the Indian Mutiny.

At time of his death in 1915, he was Hon Colonel of the 5th Bn. Somerset Light Infantry and, despite being over 80, had been highly active in recruiting volunteers for the Great War.

Peter had an older brother, Henry, who died shortly after birth in 1862 and an older sister Clara who was 12 years older than him - who were both borne by Patton Snr's first wife Clara.

He was educated at Winchester and Wellington public schools and is thought to have originally learned to ice skate whilst holidaying in Switzerland.

Following the family tradition, Peter also became a soldier and was commissioned as a Lieutenant into the 3rd Batallion, Prince Albert's Somerset Light Infantry on 20th January 1894.

Very little is actually known about his early army career. He is listed in Hart's Army List for 1896 – but not in later editions…

It was noted in the press that he passed the literary examination for officer to enter the Civil service in May 1894 but, if the newspaper archives are to believed, he seems to have spent much of his time playing village cricket, winning rowing regattas and organising and playing ice hockey across Europe.

He was also involved with the motor trade as the 1911 census shows him living in Bray, Berkshire, and descibes him as the owner of a motor garage.

In the 1920s he was listed on the electoral roll as having his abode as c/o the Royal Automobile Club on Pall Mall - which was then and still is an exclusive private members' club.

This is a separate entity to the RAC vehicle recovery service which it originally set up as an associate section for the benefits of its vehicle owning members.

Patton got married in 1904 to lady called Florence Adeline Winifred Lloyd Worrall (1872-1937) and described himself as a civil engineer on the marriage certificate. The couple did not have any children and divorced in 1912.

Presumably keen not to miss out on the action at the outbreak of the Great War, Patton arranged an attachment to join the Royal Army Service Corps Special Reserve and was Gazzetted as a 2nd Lieutenant in September 1914.

He served in France between September 1914 and May 1916, being promoted to full Lieutenant in May 1915 and Captain in October 1915. He was also attached to the Serbian Army and was awarded their Order of the White Eagle.

In July 1919 after returning home from the war, Patton was attached to the Serbs working on the historical records of motor units. He retired from the army in 1921 with the rank of Major.

Patton was quite one for the ladies and was often featured in the society pages of the Tatler in 1920s and 30s in the company of various young beauties at London society occasions or at winter holiday resorts on the continent.

In 1929, he made the headlines for all the wrong reasons after breaking off a 12-month engagment to a lady called Rona Hodson (1902-1965). No reason for the break up was given but it caused quite a stir in the society columns. Miss Hodson went on to marry naval Lt Commander Morton Martin in 1933.

Patton died on 10th April 1939 aged 63 and was buried in the family plot at St Mary's Church, Stoke St Mary in Somerset, along with his mother and father.

PETER
PATTON
THE
REF.

A humorous depiction of BM Patton from a montage of caricatures of the 1921 Varsity match where Peter was referee.

The match was staged at Mürren in Switzerland on 22nd December 1921 and Oxford beat Cambridge 27-0.

The drawings were produced by noted cartoonist Alan D'Egville and appeared in "The Sketch" dated 4th January 1922.

Involvement In Ice Hockey

Patton pretty much introduced the modern game of ice hockey to Britain in 1897 when he formed the Prince's Ice Hockey club at the recently opened Prince's Ice Skating rink in London's Knightsbridge.

The Prince's rink was a good size and shape for playing ice hockey on, being rectangular with dimensions of 210 feet x 52 feet (ie 64 by 16 meters). While this was a bit on the narrow side in comparison with the modern Olympic standard size of 60m x 30m, it was an improvement on the other London rinks of the period which were circular in shape and had been designed mainly with casual promenade skating in mind.

The Prince's rink was operated on a members-only basis and membership in its early days was 10 guineas a year - which is the equivalent of around £1.000 in 2020. The venue was aimed principally at the elite of skaters who wanted to practice on uncrowded ice.

Canadian ex-pats and other keen sportsmen gravitated to the venue and the Prince's team initially played challenge matches against the other three teams that had been set up in England – Niagara, Brighton and the Royal Engineers.

In 1902 a second team - The London Canadians - also started playing at the Prince's rink and their involvement helped guide the game towards a more recognisable version of the sport with the use of a puck instead of a ball and longer sticks with flat blades rather than the rounded bandy sticks that had previously been used.

In 1903 Patton formed and became president of a five team "English Ice Hockey League" competition involving the Prince's and London Canadians teams, Argyll and Amateur Skating Club from the Hengler's rink in London and a Cambridge University team.

This was the first ever ice hockey league to be organised in Great Britain or Europe and it ran from November 1903 to February 1904. It was won by London Canadians, with Prince's finishing second.

Unfortunately, the Hengler's rink closed in the spring of 1904 and the league was not repeated. The site is now home to the famous London Palladium theatre.

On 24 January 1904 he played in the first organised ice hockey game in Europe when Prince's played a local team in Lyons and won 2–0.

Prince's, with Patton as their captain, played in the first European tournament in October 1908 which was held in the newly opended Berliner EisPalast.

They beat Club des Patineurs de Paris 3-2 in the final, having seen off the hosts Berliner Eishockey Club 1-3 in the semi final.

In 1910, Patton led the Prince's team to the gold medal as they represented Great Britain at the first ever playing of the European championships at Les Avants near Montreux in Switzerland.

They finished top of the competitive group, having beaten Germany 1-0, the hosts 5-1 and drawn 1-1 with Belgium - and with filler games against the touring Oxford Canadians team counting in the final standings.

For many years before and after the First World War, Patton continued to lead the Prince's team in European tournaments.

Their triumphs included a runners up place at the 1913 championships in St. Moritz and winning the last ever LIHG tournament at Chamonix in January 1914.

He was also heavily involved with the Oxford v Cambridge "Varsity" match which was played more or less annually – albeit with a few exceptions - from 1900 onwards. The first (more or less) proper ice hockey game between the two rivals (as opposed to outdoor bandy, which had been played much earlier) took place at Patton's home of Prince's rink in 1900 and Patton was a goal judge.

It was later played by Oxford and Cambridge winter touring sides at various locations in Swizerland for a number of years before after WW1 – mainly for purposes of convenience but also as, after Prince's closed in 1917, there was little suitable ice to be played on in England until the new rink boom of the 1930s. Patton was referee for the Varsity matches in 1912 and 1913 and reprised the role in both 1920 and 1921 when the games were restarted after the war.

Patton was again a member of the Great Britain team at the 1924 Winter Olympics at Chamonix in the French Alps. However, he was the reserve substitute netminder at the tournament and did not manage to get any ice time.

Patton made his final appearance for the GB team on 4th April 1930 when he was 54 years old in a 2-2 draw with the French national team at the Golders Green rink. He was 55 when he finally hung up his skates after a game for the London Lions on 13th October 1931.

As well as playing ice hockey, Peter Patton was a major driving force behind the scenes. He was a founding member of the International Ice Hockey Federation (IIHF) in 1908 - or the "Ligue International de Hockey sur Glace" (LIHG) as it was known when it was originally set up in Paris - and was the inaugural president of the British Ice Hockey Association (BIHA) when he helped set it up in 1914.

He was the first President of the BIHA, a position that he held for over 20 years until 1934, was briefly President of the LIHG in 1914 and was IIHF Vice President on three different occasions - 1910/11 13/14 and 1923/24.

The Prince's team that played Lyon in 1904. Patton is 2nd left on the front row. (Source La Vie En Grand Aire, 28th January 1904)

Peter Patton at a pre-Christmas session with the Sunday Club at Richmond Ice Rink in 1931. He is seen here looking very dapper between famous author Mrs Florence Kilpatrick and her daughter Dora Kilpatrick. (Source: The Tatler, 30th December 1931)

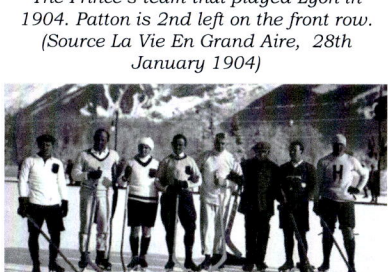

The Prince's team that won the last ever LIHG Championship at Chamonix in January 1914. Left to right: Howard Webster, Robert le Cron, Frederick Hutchinson, BM Patton, Arthur Sullivan, Matthew Agar, George Clarkson, Alfred Goodale (French Postcard)

The two teams in the first ever match to be played at the new London Ice Club in March 1927. Left to Right: Dr RN LeCron, L Percy, BJ Marden, Dr LK Lunt, Capt VH Tate, Major BM Patton, Basil Johnson, Dr FA Phillipps, General AC Critchley, G Roper, JJ Lee, Lord Charles Cavendish. (Source: The Tatler, 9th March 1927)

After retiring from playing, Patton was elected as vice-president firstly of the Streatham club and then the Wembley Lions. He was also president of the short-lived Public Schools Ice Hockey Club .

In recognition of his vast contribution to the sport of ice hockey, Peter Patton was inducted to the British Ice Hockey Hall of Fame in 1950 and to the IIHF Hall of Fame in 2002.

Besides ice hockey, Patton was a superb ice dancer and won numerous competitions. He also enjoyed skiing and was a founding member of the International Bobsleigh and Tobogganing Federation in 1923.

Patton Biography compiled by Paul Breeze, Editor of Ice Hockey Review, September 2020 from a variety of sources, including:

Gordon, David S & Harris, Martin C: Lion In Winter (Ayr & London: British Ice Hockey Heritage Publications, 2019)
Hart, Lt-Gen HG: Hart's Army List For 1896 (London: John Murray, 1896)
London Gazette (London: Various dates)
Harris, Martin C: The British Ice Hockey Hall of Fame Paperback (The History Press, 3 Dec. 2007)
Patton, Major BM: "Ice Hockey" (London: Routledge, 1936)
http://curlinghistory.blogspot.com/2017/01/curling-at-princes-skating-club-in.html
http://internationalhockeywiki.com/ihw/index.php?title=Peter_Patton
wikipedia.org/wiki/Peter_Patto
https://internationalhockey.fandom.com/wiki/Early_British_champions
https://en.wikipedia.org/wiki/Peter_Patton
https://oxforduniversityicehockey.com/the-varsity-match/
www.findmypast.co.uk, www.britishnewspaperarchive.co.uk

THE PATTON CUP

Peter Patton presented two British ice hockey trophies in his name.

Patton Cup #1

The first Patton Cup was presented to the winners of the Varsity Match between Cambridge and Oxford universities from 1927 until 2016, when it was replaced by the King Edward VII Cup.

The Patton Cup replaced the Wengen Cup, which had been presented to the winners since 1910 but went missing after the First World War.

Somewhat oddly, this replacement trophy also disappeared in the 1960s – not due to anything particularly sinister but a mix up during the changeovers of club presidents. The cup apparently lay forgotten about in a box in somebody's garage for number of years until it was finally re-discovered and returned to its proper place at the Varsity matches .

Another bizarre twist was to see the Patton Cup disappear from view again in 2014, following a player eligibility dispute within the Oxford University club and this story was related to us by Cambridge Blues head coach, Eskimos player and poet Professor Bill Harris.

It seems that Oxford won the cup that year but Cambridge did not know at the time that the Oxford Blues had disaffiliated themselves from the Oxford University Sports Federation and that Oxford University no longer considered them as an official University team so, technically, it wasn't a true Varsity match even though the Oxford team had billed it as such.

In 2015, Oxford established a new official team called the Oxford University Blues but the other Oxford Blues (aka the rebels) were still competing in the British Universities (BUIHA) ice hockey league as well.

Cambridge asked the rebel Blues to bring the Patton Cup to the final BUIHA match between the two teams, but the rebels, afraid of losing the cup forever if Cambridge were to win - as they were no longer considered the official Oxford team - did not do so.

Cambridge won the league game against the rebels and also won the next Varsity Match against the official OUBs - but there was no cup to present to the victors.

The situation dragged on and the rebel Oxford team refused point blank to return the Patton Cup despite pleas from both Universities so, in 2016, the two grand establishments pooled together to buy a new trophy – the King Edward VII Cup – to use as the accolade for future Varsity Matches.

Cambridge won the first playing for the new cup against the OUBs in 2016 and have retained it for the past three years in 2017,18 and 19. During this period, the rebel Blues faded away as a BUIHA league team and actually folded in 2017.

There were real fears that the Patton Cup might be lost forever but then, in 2019, it suddenly re-appeared at the Hockey Hall of Fame in Toronto, Canada, and a photo was published showing it being presented to the curator of the collection Phil Pritchard by some members of the rebel Oxford team.

Initial attempts by representatives of both Oxford and Cambridge Universities to have the cup returned have so far failed and it still resides "across the pond" but it is, at least, now in relatively safe hands.

Patton Cup #2

A separate Patton Cup was presented to the winners of the 1930 British Championship which saw an end of season play off competition culminating in a north v south final between Patton's own team - the London Lions - and Glasgow. (See Appendix 1 for more details).

Attempts to repeat the British Championship in 1931 were thwarted by a lack of suitable ice time and team unavailabilty and that version of the Patton Cup was never played for again.

The silver Patton Cup that was first presented to the winners of the annual Oxford v Cambridge match in 1927 by BM Patton.

The cup is engraved with the wording:

"INTER VARSITY ICE HOCKEY MATCH

Presented at St Moritz

By Major "Peter" Patton

January 1927"

The winners for each year and the scoreline are listed around the base.

After some hair raising adventures of its own, the historic cup is now safely in the hands of the (Ice) Hockey Hall of Fame in Toronto, Canada.

(Photo by HHOF.com)

Oxford's 1955 winning team with the Patton Cup. They beat Cambridge 29-0 at Richmond Ice Rink - a record score for the Varsity series. Interestingly enough, Frederick Meredith – highly regarded BIHA President in the 1980s and early 90s - was in goal for Cambridge and is reported to have done a good job in keeping the score from being even higher. (Source: Puckstruck.com)

THE EIHL PATTON CONFERENCE

In 2017 the British Elite Ice Hockey League named its third conference in Patton's honour.

The new Patton Conference operated in an interlocking format alongside the existing Erhardt and Gardiner Conferences, which had also been named after British ice hockey personalities of the past.

The Erhardt Conference was dedicated to Carl Erhardt (1897-1988) – captain of the GB team that won the ice hockey gold medal at the 1936 Winter Olympics – while the mainly Scottish-based Gardiner Conference was named after former Chicago Black Hawks NHL netminder Charlie Gardiner (1904-1934) who had originally been born in Edinburgh.

The inaugural 2017/18 Patton Conference was won by Manchester Storm who were presented with the EIHL's new Patton Trophy. The Storm also finished runners up in the Elite League overall.

The 2018/19 season Patton Conference was won by the Guildford Flames. The following 2019/20 league season was not completed due to the coronavirus pandemic and no titles were awarded.

The Manchester Storm team celebrate winning the 2017/18 EIHL Patton Conference - with a new "Patton Trophy" (Photo by Mark Ferriss, All Sports Photography)

ICE-HOCKEY

By

MAJOR PATTON

Past President of the
British Ice-Hockey Association

LONDON
GEORGE ROUTLEDGE & SONS LTD.
BROADWAY HOUSE: 68–74 CARTER LANE, E.C.
1936

FOREWORD

I AM deeply indebted to many friends in this country and in Canada for valuable assistance and information.

It is quite impossible to mention here all those who have so very kindly helped me, but I should like to take this opportunity to thank them all, and especially the following :

The Lady Dorothy Mills, the well-known traveller and writer, for her advice and early help ; the Hon. Sir Arthur Stanley, G.B.E., C.B., M.V.O., for the ' Royal Hockey Match ' and for ' Some Early Days in Canada ' ; Monsieur Paul Loicq, President of the International Ice-Hockey League, for reading the chapter on the History of the League ; Mr. P. V. Hunter, C.B.E., and Mr. J. F. Ahearne, President and Secretary respectively of the B.I.H.A., for assistance in many ways ; Mr. J. R. Gilmour, Hon. Secretary, Scottish Ice-Hockey Association, for information about the history of the game in Scotland ; Mr. F. A. de Marwicz, for reading the chapter on 'Varsity Hockey ; Mr. T. G. Cannon, for letting me have an illustration of the early days of Ice-Hockey ; Mr. J. J. Cawthra, for information about the earliest 'Varsity hockey matches ; Colonel Arthur Sullivan, K.C., for notes about the early history ; Mr. G. C. Cowan, Oxford, and Mr. P. H. Holmes, Cambridge, the respective 'Varsity captains, for loan of Minute Books ; Monsieur Maurice Andreossi, St. Moritz ; Mr. Arnold Lunn ; Dr. F. A. Phillipps, M.D. ; and Mr. E. Leacock.

'PETER' B. M. PATTON.

CONTENTS

CHAPTER I

SOME ACCOUNTS OF THE EARLY DAYS OF THE GAME IN CANADA AND HOW THE STANLEY CUP CAME TO BE GIVEN

FOR very valuable accounts of Canada's earliest hockey days the author is extremely indebted to Sir Arthur Stanley and J. J. Cawthra.[1] The latter, who lives in Toronto, recently called on the Sporting Editor of *The Evening Telegram*, Toronto's best sporting paper, who very kindly let him copy some notes from a publication called *The All Sports Record Book* which the paper considers as probably quite authentic. Jack Cawthra wrote the author : " You will note that Hockey goes back to 1879, I think myself that 1879 would be about correct. The game you mention as played at Kingston Harbour in 1888 is too modern. I played as a boy here in Toronto in 1889-90, and it was well established then."

From the very interesting notes it would appear that Ice-Hockey is an offshoot of English Field Hockey. The notes from *The All Sports Record Book* are as follows :—

" Ice-Hockey was first played in Montreal in December 1879.

" First regulations for game were drawn by R. F. Smith, resident of Montreal—at that time a student at McGill University. In a letter written by Smith he quotes as follows :—

" ' In the summer of 1879, W. F. Robertson of McGill University, a friend of mine, went to England and was impressed with Field Hockey, he was a skating enthusiast ; and when he returned to Montreal, he explained the principles of the sport to me, and asked if I could figure out some way that it could be played on ice. As a result, I

[1] J. J. Cawthra, founder of the Inter-'Varsity match. See 'Varsity History.

drew up the first set of Hockey rules and submitted them
to Robertson and some fellow-students at McGill on 17th
September 1879.

" ' I used some Field Hockey rules, a few others I
thought out myself, and mixed in some Rugby Football
rules, the latter being the reason why Hockey is an
" Onside Game."

" ' The first Hockey game was played on river ice in
December 1879. Nine men a side was the proper number,
but thirty undergrads turned up with all kinds of sticks.

" ' A square puck was used. The core was cut out of
a hard rubber ball and then squared off. During the
winter of 1879-1880 Inter-Class matches were played.

" ' During the winter 1880-81, the first team was organized and was called McGill University Hockey Club. It
was first introduced into Ottawa some five years later by
A. P. Low, formerly of McGill and a member of the original
team.' "

Sir Arthur Stanley has contributed the following very
interesting information about the part Lt.-Col. Ward, K.C.
(Judge Ward), and others took in Canada's early hockey
days. Col. Ward and other political notabilities of the
early 'eighties formed the first organized team in Ontario.
The team played at Lindsay, Ottawa, Kingston and
Toronto. One of the members of the team, J. G. A.
Creighton, in answer to a letter from Col. Ward of about
ten years ago asking for information about old-time
hockey, wrote the Colonel that he had the honour to be
captain of the team of the first regular hockey club to be
formed in Canada, which was at Montreal in 1877.[1]

How the Stanley Cup came to be given

Col. Ward also asked the late J. A. Barron, K.C., for
information. The latter mentioned how Col. Colville,
A.D.C. to Lord Stanley, came to him in the House one
afternoon in 1893 and said that Lord Stanley wished to

---

[1] There thus seems to be little difference between the dates given
by R. F. Smith and J. G. A. Creighton respectively.

present a cup to promote Ice-Hockey in Ontario, and would he and H. A. Ward and Sidney Fisher go into Ontario and play some games, which they did. An incident in one of these matches would be interesting to relate but lack of space prevents. J. A. Barron was the star player of the Parliamentary team which played many pleasant games with the Government House team.

' THE REBELS ' CLUB

On arriving at Rideau in 1888, where Lord Stanley of Preston, the Governor of Canada, resided, the Hon. Arthur Stanley, his third son, was at once greatly attracted by Ice-Hockey, which was carried on in only quite a small way.

The games were then being played on the public skating rink in Montreal and Mr. Arthur Stanley and his brothers, including the present Lord Derby, took part in them.

After a time the skaters began to object to the frequency of the games, with the result that play was given up there and a private club was formed by Mr. Arthur Stanley, which used the open-air rink in the grounds of Rideau Hall. The club was called ' The Rebels,' and in describing their kit Sir Arthur said: '' We wore red shirts and white trousers, which would have been quite in the fashion nowadays ! ''

FORMATION OF THE ONTARIO HOCKEY ASSOCIATION

In 1890, Mr. Arthur Stanley conceived the idea of forming an Ice-Hockey Association, and with two or three friends called a meeting to put the scheme in being. As the result of the meeting which was largely attended, the Ontario Hockey Association was formed ; consequently the real founder of this body was the present Hon. Sir Arthur Stanley.

It will be a very long time, if ever, before the unique record of this family is equalled ; a family so distinguished in the annals of Ice-Hockey and even more so in the affairs of life ' that count.'

CHAPTER II

VERY EARLY ENGLISH ICE-HOCKEY GAMES

Now and then one hears of this or that sport being described as the Sport of Kings. That this epitaph can to a very moderate extent be applied to Ice-Hockey is quite true.

ICE-HOCKEY MATCH AT BUCKINGHAM PALACE IN 1895

Extremely few people know that hockey on the ice has been played by Royalty. However, in that very hard weather of 1895, which began on January 6th and lasted well into March, a most interesting match was played on the lake at Buckingham Palace.

Strictly speaking, the game more resembled bandy, as played in those days, than hockey ; bandy sticks being used with the puck instead of hockey sticks.

The match was between a Palace team and that of Lord Stanley.

BUCKINGHAM PALACE TEAM

The Prince of Wales (afterwards King Edward the Seventh).
The Duke of York (afterwards King George the Fifth).
Lord Mildmay.
Sir Francis Astley-Corbett, Bart.
Sir William Bromley Davenport (now Brig.-Gen., K.C.B., C.M.G., C.B.E., D.S.O.).
Mr. Ronald Moncrieff.

LORD STANLEY'S TEAM

Lord Stanley (now the Earl of Derby, K.G., G.C.B., G.C.V.O., K.C.V.O., C.B., P.C., T.D., J.P.).
The Hon. F. C. Stanley (the late Brig.-Gen., C.M.G., D.S.O.).
The Hon. G. F. Stanley (now P.C., G.C.I.E., C.M.G.).

4

The Hon. A. F. Stanley (now Colonel, D.S.O.).
The Hon. F. W. Stanley (now Colonel, D.S.O.).
Lord Annally (the late).

The game had to be played early, as the Prince of Wales was attending a levee that morning. The visiting side scored numerous goals to the single one of the Palace side. The Prince was greatly impressed by the play of the Hon. F. W. Stanley, who dribbled the puck at considerable speed while skating backwards in front of the Prince.

MATCH AT NIAGARA IN THE 1896–97 SEASON

Another very interesting and unique match was played at the old Niagara Rink, now a motor establishment and close to St. James's Park Station, in the season above stated.

Lord Derby (then Lord Stanley) and five of his brothers played the Niagara team and beat them very easily. The Hon. V. A. Stanley (the late Admiral the Hon. Sir Victor Stanley, K.C.B., M.V.O.), who did not play in the Palace match, made the sixth brother of the team, consequently the team was wholly a family one. The Hon. Sir Arthur Stanley, G.B.E., C.B., M.V.O., the present treasurer to St. Thomas's Hospital, was the best player of all the seven brothers, but was unable to take part in either of these two games. An attack of rheumatic fever a year or two previous to the Palace one, prevented him, it is extremely to be regretted, from ever playing again, and has been a very great handicap to him ever since.

Lord Derby and all his brothers, except the Admiral, were at Wellington College ; in both matches, therefore, except for one member in the Palace game, the visiting sides were composed entirely of students, past and present, from this famous Berkshire school.

MATCH AT NIAGARA, JANUARY 1ST, 1899

This was another match in which members of Lord Derby's family took part. An old Wellingtonian side, composed of the Hon. A. F. Stanley, the Hon. F. W. Stanley,

Messrs. R. and J. Gossett, and the author played a Niagara team at that rink.

The latter side won, although the ' O.W.'s ' led 2—0 for a considerable period of the game.

The Stanley brothers had not played for quite a long time, and the Gossett brothers, though members of the Princes Ice-Hockey Club, only played very occasionally. Gradually Niagara, the fitter team, wore down the ' O.W.'s ' to win 3—2.

The most prominent players on the Niagara side were J. H. H. Nation (now Brig.-Gen., D.S.O., M.P.), P. Platt and the Hon. S. R. Beresford (the late).

CHAPTER III

GLIMPSES OF ENGLISH ICE-HOCKEY HISTORY FROM 1895 TO 1936

1895

ROYAL hockey match at Buckingham Palace in January, probably.

1895-96

Ice-Hockey at Niagara.

On November 7th, 1896, Princes Ice-Skating Club was opened, and Princes Ice-Hockey Club formed on December 23rd, probably. Some of the founders : C. I. Napier, C. and R. French Brewster, Vane Pennell and the author.

1896-97

January 4th. First hockey practice. February 13th. First match.—Princes 6 v. Fenwick's team 3. Princes team : C. and R. French-Brewster, Vane Pennell, B. M. Patton, The late Hon. Algernon Grosvenor (goal).

1897-98

Various matches played at and between Princes and Niagara and scratch teams.

1898-99

Similar matches to previous season, and also a match at Brighton on January 4th, 1899, when Princes lost 4—2 to the home team on the circular rink in that town.

1899-1900

Various matches between Princes, Niagara and Brighton. Princes also played several matches with the R.E.'s from

Chatham, in whose team there was a Carr-Harris, the first of quite a number of members of that Canadian family to play hockey in England up to recent years. On March 16th, the first 'Varsity match was played at Princes. See 'Varsity History.

1900–01

Matches at Princes against various scratch teams. On January 22nd, 1901, we stopped hockey practice game at 7.25 on death of Queen Victoria being announced.

1901–02

Princes won all matches except for losing two and drawing one against Cambridge.

1902–03

Notable season. London Canadians Club formed and they taught us hockey. Their team was Donald Hingston (capt.), son of a very famous surgeon, the late Sir William Hingston ; Arthur Sullivan (secretary), son of the late Sir William Sullivan, Chief Justice of Prince Edward Island ; Keith Edgar of the R.E., Chatham, son of the late Sir James Edgar, at one time Speaker of the Canadian House of Commons ; F. F. Carr-Harris from Ontario, also of the R.E.'s at Chatham ; S. D. Mackenzie (the late) and G. Furlong.

February 6th, 1903, was the date of the first match ever played in England between two Canadian teams and under Canadian rules. The Canadian Rugby team on tour beat the London Canadians 5—3. Matches between Henglers, London Canadians and Princes were frequent. The Canadians beat Princes for the Princes Challenge Cup in the final match for that trophy after extra time.

1903–04

A more notable season than last. The first Ice-Hockey League was formed and a schedule of fixtures drawn up. Five teams took part. London Canadians won with

14 points, Princes 2nd with 12, Argyll (Henglers) 3rd, Amateur Skating Club (Henglers) 4th, and Cambridge 5th. The Princes team went to Davos in January 1904 and won the Bandy Tournament there, and then on to Lyons to play in the first hockey match staged at that rink, which Princes won.

On February 4th, 1904, a match was played at Henglers on the occasion of the Union Jack Club Carnival, and is the only one which has been witnessed by Royalty in this country. The match was Internationals v. London. The former just won. The Internationals were some of the ten players that went to Davos and Lyons. A. Sullivan, C. E. Vernon (the late), C. M. G. Howell (the late), C. F. Clayton and B. M. Patton (capt.). London team : D. H. Hingston, A. G. von Berg, K. Edgar, C. I. Napier, T. G. Cannon (capt.) ; the last two named were also Internationals.

1904–05

November 26th. London Canadians beat Princes ; last match, as the Canadian players scattered afterwards.

Princes team went to Lyons again and won 7—0.

1905–06

January 30th. Lyons team came to Princes. Home team won 9—1. Princes team went to Lyons and won and also beat Paris in Paris.

In March, Princes played two matches with the newly formed Oxford Canadian team.

1906–07

A number of International matches were played this season as well as several between Princes and the Oxford Canadians, all of which Princes won except the Cup match in March, which the Canadians won 8—4. Princes went to Grindelwald in January 1907, and won the Grindelwald Challenge Cup. Two matches were played with the ' Sporting Club de Lyon,' in February, one in London and the other in Lyons. Princes won both games. By winning

in Lyons the handsome challenge trophy, a bronze statue
of David, became the English team's property as it was its
third successive victory.   Princes beat the Club des
Patineurs in Brussels and at Princes on March 10th, with
an ' A ' team, by 17 goals to 1 ; an ' A ' team played the
Belgians as the first team had met the Oxford Canadians
that evening. Of the 17 goals, C. M. G. Howell scored 15,
an individual record that has never been eclipsed in this
country ; it would be very interesting to know if a player
in any other country has beaten it.

1907–08

Princes won the Grindelwald Challenge Cup again, also
won matches at Leysin, Villars-sur-Allons, but lost in Lyons
by the odd goal in 9 and drew with Paris. Won most of the
matches against the Oxford Canadians, and near the end of
the season played two matches in Brussels against different
teams and won both.

1908–09

Early in the season Princes represented England in the
first International Ice-Hockey Tournament ever organized
in Berlin after a very hard final match against France, who
had previously beaten the German team by a much larger
margin than the English team had.   It was at this
Tournament that H. Kleeberg, who organized it, and the
author, began what has now been a very long friendship.

In January 1909, Princes won the Grindelwald Cup for
the third time, beat a Swiss Romande Ligue Team but lost
to La Villa Club at Lausanne.

January 23-24. The Championship of the International
Ice-Hockey took place at Chamonix and was won by
England, represented by Princes. The final match against
France was only won after forty minutes over time ! and no
reserves allowed in those days, of course.

1909–10

This season was notable as it was the first occasion that
the Championship of Europe was played for. Ice con-

ditions were extremely bad all three days. January 10-12. Belgium, England, Germany and Switzerland were the four competing countries, but the Oxford Canadians were *hors Concours* ; they merely played to give the spectators the chance of seeing how a Canadian team did play. The English team beat Switzerland and Germany and drew with Belgium. England, by not losing a match, whereas the other three countries had all lost matches to each other, won the title of European Champions. English team was T. O. M. Sopwith, goal ; B. M. Patton (capt.) and B. C. Cox, backs ; H. H. Duden, R. N. Le Cron and J. Cox, forwards. England was lucky to win, because two of her best players, A. N. Macklin and R. D. Nolan, were not available. The former, who had only just recovered the use of an arm broken in a match in Paris a month previously, broke his knee-cap a few days previous to the Championship. R. D. Nolan broke a rib in a practice match two days before the first match and H. Duden had to play with his shoulder strapped up, it had a broken bone in it as the result also of the Paris match.

On March 26th, England beat Scotland 11—1 at Princes, the first match ever played between them.

1910–11

Princes lost to Scotland in Glasgow 8—3, at the Crossmyloof rink, which had a bandstand on pillars in the centre of the rink. The London Club lost to Manchester 5—3, in that town next day. On December 27th, Princes beat the first German team to visit England by 8—3, at Princes. Princes visited Les Avants in Switzerland in January ; beat Switzerland and Belgium, lost to Germany and the Oxford Canadians, but at Chamonix just afterwards with several players injured lost to the last three named countries.

1911–12

Not an eventful season. In December, Princes visited Paris but lost 7—3. Four of the best Princes players assisted Louis Dufour, a leading light in Switzerland's early hockey days, to win the Swiss Championship for Les Avants. The players were the late M. E. Batting (goalkeeper), R. N. Le Cron, A. A. Sullivan (who had returned from Canada for a holiday) and the author (forwards).

1912–13

Princes won an International Tournament at Les Avants early in 1913. On January 14th, as the result of previous steps taken by Lord Carberry, H. H. Duden and the author (all members of Princes Ice-Hockey Club), in conjunction with the Hon. F. N. Curzon of St. Moritz Bandy Club, a club was formed called St. Moritz Bandy and Ice-Hockey Club. This is how Ice-Hockey came to be introduced into the Engadine and at St. Moritz, which, like Davos, had hitherto been a stronghold of bandy.

An International Ice-Hockey Tournament was then organized by the writer. Five countries took part. After a number of close games, Germany beat England 5—4 to win premier honours ; England gained second place.

1913–14

This winter the British Ice-Hockey Association was first organized. Cambridge, Manchester, Oxford Canadians, R.E.'s (Chatham) and Princes were the composing Clubs. B. M. Patton was made President and T. G. Cannon, Hon. Secretary and Treasurer.

Princes, representing England, sent a very strong team to Les Avants to play in an International Tournament there, which it won, and then on to Chamonix for the Championship of the International Ice-Hockey League, which England also won.

1920–21

After the 'Varsity match at Mürren in December 1920, the author took some players from both teams to St. Moritz, where they were joined by G. E. Clarkson, who played for England in 1914, to play for the Bouvier Cup, which the Englishmen won.

1921–22

In February, the European Championship and an International Ice-Hockey Tournament were organized at St. Moritz by the author in conjunction with the St. Moritz Ice-Hockey Club and Swiss Ice-Hockey officials. The English team, composed of five players from the famous Oxford team (see 'Varsity History) with the author in goal, won the International Tournament, but could not take part in the European Championship as the 'Varsity men were not English born. The Kulm Cup was awarded to the Englishmen for their victory.

1922–23

A British Army team composed of. Canadian officers visited St. Moritz and played several matches. Some of the members of the team assisted the author with one or two other players to win the Kulm Cup by defeating Davos, the only other team to enter the competition for the Cup.

1923–24

Olympic Hockey, as recorded in Olympic History, was the outstanding event this season.

1924–25

This season was noticeable for the first appearance of B. N. Sexton's famous team, the London Lions. They made a very successful debut at St. Moritz and won all their matches there except one.

1925–26

The ' Lions ' again came to St. Moritz this winter and were equally successful. The English team that competed for the European Championship at Davos in January was almost entirely composed of members of the Lions team. England would have probably gained a higher place than fourth if any reserves had been available. In England's match against Switzerland, the eventual winners of the Championship, overtime had to be played for twenty minutes; the lack of reserves caused us to lose 4—3.

1926–27

In December 1926, Princes Club was re-formed and took a team to St. Moritz, where Davos was played. Injuries caused several members of the English team to be absent from this match, so Davos won 8—0.

The Ice Club, Westminster, which was opened this season, was the venue of the first match ever played in England by a team from Canada. The English team, however, with the exception of one of the two goalkeepers, was composed of Canadians resident in the country. The Montreal Victorias led 12—0 at the end of the second period. In the third period, when the other English goal-keeper was playing, was a much more even one; the visitors only scored twice more, and B. N. Sexton, the English captain, got our one and only goal in reply.

In April a Belgian team came to the Ice Club and lost a good game against England by 3—1.

1927–28

This was a very busy hockey season at the Ice Club where numerous inter-club matches were played. An English team went to Vienna in January 1928, and also took part in the Olympic Hockey matches. (See Olympic Hockey.)

In March the Canadian Olympic team played England at the Ice Club and won 11—4. In April there was another England v. Belgium match at the Ice Club, which the home team won.

1928–29

In November the St. Moritz team came to London for the first time and drew with a B.I.H.A. team at the Ice Club.

In December, Richmond Rink opened, and on the 26th the first hockey match was played there ; Services 4, B. N. Sexton's team 4.

In January 1929, a B.I.H.A. team visited St. Moritz, Prague, Vienna and Budapest.

In March, German and Swedish teams visited England, the latter for the first time, and the match with whom, at Richmond, caused quite a stir in certain journals owing to a certain amount of roughish play.

1929–30

Ice-Hockey became much more general this season as there were four other rinks where the game was played : Golders Green, Park Lane Ice Club, Hammersmith and Hove.

A B.I.H.A. team visited St. Moritz and, as England, played in the World Championship matches at Chamonix in January 1930. Bad weather prevented the completion of the schedule of matches. As the English team did not go to Berlin, where the remaining matches were played, she was unplaced.

A notable event of the season was the first visit to Europe of a Japanese team, which, after playing in the World Championship, visited London and played against England at Hammersmith, and Cambridge at the Ice Club, but lost to the former 7—1 and to the latter 4—3.

The Canadas, who had also played at Chamonix, came to England and played at Hove and Golders Green in February.

In addition to a large number of league matches, St. Moritz visited London again in March and France in April. One of the last matches of the season at the Ice Club was the decisive one for the Junior League Championship, which was won by Princes II, who became the first holders of the Hunter Cup ; the donor was a member of the winning team.

The season was very prolonged, and not until May 17th was the final match played for the Patton Cup, which was won by the London Lions, who beat Glasgow 2—1.

1930–31

A still busier season than its predecessor. Early in November a German team visited London and played four matches against England, winning one, losing one and drawing two. The Germans also played against Oxford and won 2—1.

An English team visited Arosa and St. Moritz and then went to Krynica to play in the World and European Championships. England lost her first match, which was to Austria, after thirty minutes over time, and Austria went on to win the European Championship. ' Dicky,' Baron H. Trauttenberg, the popular Cambridge captain in 1931, and who has been playing for Streatham for several seasons, was the Austrian captain and still is.

In March the Canadian team which had won at Krynica played matches in England on their way home.

This season was also a very prolonged one. The final match was between Lions and Queen's at the Bayswater rink on May 14th.

1931–32

The season started very early. The Grosvenor House Canadians was formed at the Park Lane Ice Club, and played in the first match at the newly opened rink in Paris, and a few days afterwards, on October 13th, a London team also went there. A German team played three matches in London between October 11th and 16th.

Early in January 1932, a Scottish I.H. League team played several matches in London. On January 18th, the Ottawas, the Canadian team that was touring Europe, met England at Grosvenor House. This match was the first one to be broadcast in this country but the result must have disappointed those who listened-in, as the home team lost 7—0. There were two other very notable events this season. The Inter-'Varsity match was played in England for the first time and Walter Browne, now so well known and popular over here, brought over the forerunner of the several teams that have visited this country from Boston,

U.S.A. After a couple of good matches with England teams they left for the Continent.

The Zurich team arrived about the end of February and won two out of three matches with England teams.

On March 4th, Oxford, this season's League winners, beat ' The Rest ' at Oxford 2—1.

England took part in the European Championship in Berlin but was not very successful. Gerry Davey, then seventeen years of age, made his initial appearance for England in this event and was our ' star ' player. The Boston team played two more even games with England on March 23rd and 24th on the way home and won both. Between April 7th and 16th the Austrian team played six matches with England, winning two, losing one, and drawing two at various rinks in this country.

1932–33

The Racing Club de Paris played two matches against England team in London, in October, which were drawn, but beat Oxford.

Early in November, the German team played England at Purley and lost 2—1, and at Streatham, where the match was drawn, but also lost 6—1 to the Grosvenor House Canadians.

In November the Edmonton Superiors beat the South of England twice and Oxford.

A B.I.H.A. team played matches in Paris and at Arosa and Klosters at the end of December.

On January 23rd, 1933, England experienced very hard luck in not beating the Edmontons at Hammersmith, as the latter only equalised just on ' time.'

The Torontos played several matches against England in February and March and won all, but England beat the Boston Rangers in one match out of three ; this was at Southampton on April 7th.

The chief events of the season, however, were two matches between the American and the Canadian teams on March 27th and April 6th ; each country won a game.

In the match on March 27th, between Boston Rangers

and Streatham which was a draw, two referees officiated for the first time in this country.

Oxford were again League Champions this season.

1933-34

In October, Austria beat England 5—4 and the Grosvenor House Canadians 3—1.

In November, France beat England at Hammersmith and Streatham.

The Ottawa team beat England 7—0 at Streatham in November, and Queens, who had a very good team this season, beat the Paris Volants 4—2 at Queens. Queens had an extremely successful continental tour this winter, and F. le Blanc was their outstanding player.

Walter Browne again brought a team from Boston and played four matches in January with England teams ; three were drawn but the U.S.A. team won the other 2—0.

During the first fortnight in February, England took part in the World and European Championships in Milan, beat Roumania and Italy but lost a vital match to Austria.

The Saskatoon Quakers, who had represented Canada in the World Championship just referred to, played other matches on the Continent but did not visit England.

Grosvenor House Canadians, League Champions this season, drew 'The Rest' 7—7 at Grosvenor House on March 28th.

1934-35

The opening of the Empire Pool, Wembley, in October gave Ice-Hockey a very great prominence this season. It was the first rink in this country to be built thoroughly up to date in every way as regards hockey requirements and to accommodate a large crowd.

On October 27th, a novelty as regards Ice-Hockey took place ; teams of six a side played each other five minutes each way at Wembley ; Streatham was the eventual winner.

The International Club Tournament was instituted this season and played in two groups with two French and two

English teams in each.   It made a very interesting addition to the season's schedule of matches.

Hockey in this country was of a much higher standard than ever before.   Several new clubs were formed—the Richmond Hawks, the Wembley Lions, the Wembley Canadians.

England had hard luck in not winning the European Championship at Davos.   She came out second, losing to Switzerland, the winning country, by a narrow margin.

The Winnipeg Monarchs, winners of the World's Championship at Davos in February, played some matches in England at the end of this month and during the first fortnight in March.   Of these they lost two to Wembley and one to England but also beat England once.

Other teams from the Continent to visit England, apart from those playing in the International Club Tournament, were Munich, Prague and Davos.

Streatham had a very successful season and won both the National Championship and the International Club Tournament.   The Club experienced only one defeat during the season, and that a very narrow one, 1—0 by the Winnipeg Monarchs.

1935–36

This season was by far the biggest and most important one hitherto.

Hockey was further helped by the opening of another up-to-date big rink, the Empress Stadium, Earl's Court, which could accommodate a very large number of spectators.   This rink was the home of two new teams, the Earl's Court Rangers and the Kensington Corinthians.

The outstanding event was, of course, England's Olympic success.   (See Olympic History.)

Broadcasting was a big feature ; especially so was an outstanding one by Bob Bowman of the Olympic match at Garmisch between Canada and England.

The remarkable attendances at hockey matches at the newly opened Sports Drome at Brighton was another very notable feature.   There were very greatly increased attendances at Wembley, Streatham and Richmond compared with last year. The 'House Full' notice was frequently in evidence.

Enormously increased Press publicity during the season; a certain evening paper on one occasion had a heading right across the top of the page: " Ice-Hockey Now a National Game."

Some firms used Ice-Hockey as a means of advertising. A certain brewery had a life-size picture of a player in action.

For the first time a weekly paper was published devoted exclusively to Ice-Hockey, *The Ice Hockey World*, by R. Giddens, who played for and coached Streatham the previous season.

The intervals between the periods in matches were on the whole far more interesting than last season. In addition to novel entertainments, our Olympic skaters frequently very kindly gave exhibitions, in addition many high-class displays by other skaters.

Towards the end of the season a film exclusvely devoted to Ice-Hockey was made, the first of its kind.

Wembley Lions followed Streatham's example of the previous season by winning both the major leagues. Interest in the National League was sustained up to the very last match of the season, when Wembley Canadians beat Streatham; had Streatham been the victors they would have won the Championship again. As it was, Lions beat the Richmond Hawks for first place on goal average only.

In Birmingham, Ice-Hockey scored a very great success by reason of the wonderful successes record of the Birmingham Maple Leafs, who won the English League.

In the semi-final of the International League at Wembley on March 16th, there was one English and one French referee. This will probably be a regular occurrence in the future for matches of this kind.

The very great popularity of the Test Matches in December, and the running of excursion trains from Northampton to London for matches at Wembley were other notable features of the season.

Want of space curtails further reference to Ice-Hockey

during the past winter ; a whole book could be written about it.

The number of matches played this season in England reached a total of 270, an easy record.

National League	84
London Paris Tournament	53
Channel Cup	5
London Cup	30
English League	23
Exhibition Matches	75
	270

CHAPTER IV

SCOTTISH ICE-HOCKEY

By J. R. GILMOUR

ICE-HOCKEY was first played in Scotland about the year 1908 at the old rink at Crossmyloof, Glasgow, on which site the present rink stands. Hockey in those far-off days was far more difficult than it is to-day, as the players of twenty-eight years ago had certain structural obstacles to overcome in the form of the iron supports which raised themselves from the middle of the rink to give support to the roof—these pillars also served the purpose of supporting a balcony which was built around them to house an orchestra which provided the skaters with the music necessary for their evolutions. The ice surface for hockey was only some 140′ × 49′, no nets were provided, and short sticks, after the fashion of bandy sticks, were used by the players (imagine how the modern player would scoff at such equipment !).

Towards the end of the season 1908–1909 a game was played at the Princes Rink, in London, between a Scottish team and an English one, and the game was rated as an International, but Scotland fared badly and suffered defeat to the tune of 11 goals to 1. The following season a return game was arranged and took place at Crossmyloof. The Scots, who had discovered in the previous game at London that their short sticks were really of little use, had in the meantime put in much assiduous practice with the longer stick as was used by the Englishmen, and the result of the game, 6—1 in favour of the Scots, shows that their labours were not in vain.

This original rink at Crossmyloof finally closed in February 1918 and was in a state of comparative neglect until early in 1928, when a body of gentlemen, keen curlers all, gathered together with the firm resolve to build another Ice Rink, with the result that the Scottish Ice Rink Co. (1928) Ltd. was formed. They selected for their site, as already mentioned, that on which the old rink stood, and the present rink is known as the Scottish Ice Rink.

Constituting the Directorship of the Scottish Ice Rink Co. (1928) were representatives of curling and skating interests, among the latter being the late Lady Yarrow. It was among these directors that Scottish Ice-Hockey found two great friends and champions for the great 'cause,' as will become apparent at a later stage in this narrative.

With the advent of the rink and a fine hard winter during the months of November and December 1928, some Glaswegians and Canadians resident in the city became acquainted as the result of a series of outdoor hockey games played at Bearsden, Dunbartonshire, and at Ardinning Loch, Strathblane, and four enthusiasts of their number had a meeting early in December 1928 with the Manager appointed to the rink, Mr. James Gourley. These four enthusiasts were J. C. (Stewie) Lindsay and Hugh W. Reid, both Canadians, J. R. Gilmour (now Hon. Secretary of the Scottish Ice-Hockey Association, and Captain Scottish team 1932 and 1933), and G. C. Scott (later a Rugby International trialist). Little headway was made with the rink management at first to grant facilities to stage the game, but with the official opening of the rink early in January 1929, a meeting was called of all interested in the game, and it was at this meeting that the players found two great allies in Mr. Frank Stuart (Chairman of the rink Directors) and Mr. Andrew Mitchell (also a Director and donor of the Mitchell Trophy). These two gentlemen have done so much for the game in Scotland that they are best described as the Fathers of Scottish Ice-Hockey. A second meeting was called in February 1929, and was an overwhelming success. At that meeting Mr. Frank Stuart was appointed President of the Association, Mr. Andrew Mitchell was appointed Vice-President, and it is of interest to note that these gentlemen still hold these positions. The meeting also appointed Mr. D. B. A. Carty, Hon. Secretary and Treasurer, a position which was later split into two offices, but Mr. Carty remained in his position as Hon. Secretary until the season 1933–1934. No more energetic or suitable a person could have been chosen for the post, and much of the success of the game in Scotland is due to Mr. Carty's valiant efforts.

Ten clubs joined this first meeting of the Association, and they were Glasgow Canadians, Bearsden, Bridge of Weir, Doonside (Ayrshire), Achtungs, Queens, Dennistoun, Kelvingrove, Glasgow Skating Club, and Scottish Corinthians (who dropped out at the end of the season). In the two latter Clubs, it is interesting to note, were some players who had played on the old rink, notably Messrs. H. R. Orr, J. Ritchie, D. M'Gill (who refereed the Scottish-English at Crossmyloof in 1910 and who still renders valuable assistance to hockey) and J. B. Wharrie, who kept goal against England in 1910.

For the remainder of the season 1929, bounce games were played and the Association did not really get into its stride until the season 1929–30, with the following clubs forming the active membership of the Association, Bearsden, Queens, Doonside, Kelvingrove, Achtungs, Glasgow Skating Club, Bridge of Weir, Glasgow University, Dennistoun and Mohawks. The Association decided that there were too many clubs to run in one division, and it was decided to seed the clubs by running them in one division for the first half of the season, the first five forming the first division and the second five the second division ; the teams finished in this order :—

	Pld.	Won	Lost	Drn.	Goals For	Agst.	Pts.
Bearsden . .	4	4	0	0	17	9	8
Achtungs . .	4	3	0	1	22	4	7
Queens . .	4	3	0	1	12	3	7
Mohawks .	4	2	2	0	16	8	4
Bridge of Weir .	4	2	2	0	8	6	4
Kelvingrove. .	4	2	2	0	10	16	4
Glasgow Skating Club . .	4	1	3	0	6	12	2
Doonside . .	4	1	3	0	6	18	2
Glasgow 'Varsity .	4	0	3	1	7	16	1
Dennistoun . .	4	0	3	1	3	15	1

At the end of this season,1929–1930, the winners of the two divisions were Mohawks, 1st division, and Kelvingrove, 2nd division, and the standard of play had improved so rapidly that the S.I.H.A. Council thought it expedient to call a general meeting of the Association to ask for clubs that would volunteer to amalgamate and so cut down the number of clubs to permit more playing time for the further benefit of the standard of play. This meeting resulted in the number of clubs being reduced to nine, with the disappearance of Doonside, whose players were absorbed in other teams.

Naturally, by this time Canadians in and around Glasgow read in the Press of the playing of their national game, and just as quickly made their appearances at the rink, where their services were in great demand. Scots puck chasers of to-day owe these Canadians of the early days much gratitude for the many hours they spent in coaching pupils who were only too keen to learn all they could about this great game, nor were they backward, for within a year or two they were actually displacing their mentors in representative sides.

The process of gradually reducing the number of teams continued slowly with each season until the present, 1935–1936, there are five clubs. Kelvingrove, Lions, Mustangs, Glasgow University and Mohawks—these teams have just finished possibly the most successful season yet. Public enthusiasm has been tremendous and packed houses have witnessed some grand struggles ; during the season just finished the highest attendances so far have been recorded.

During all this time much attention has been paid to the young idea. The ages of the youngsters playing in Scotland range from twelve to sixteen years, and they have their own association and officials, their own league and their own knock-out tournament. They have had various coaches through the years and during the last two seasons have been coached by the senior association's professional coaches. The first trophy presented to the juniors for knock-out play was a silver puck presented by D. B. A. Carty (Hon. Sec.), J. Fullerton (Captain of Mohawks) and J. R. Gilmour (then Captain of Bears)—the puck was won by Mohicans. In the early part of 1936, Mr. Norman McPherson, a hockey enthusiast, presented a handsome trophy, known as the McPherson Cup, for annual competition by knock-out play, and the first holders are Junior Mohawks (formerly Mohicans). The juniors practise for forty-five minutes every Saturday morning, and the teams presently constituting their association are Junior Mohawks, Lions, Mustangs and Kelvingrove.

This policy of encouraging the youngsters has had its due reward, as no fewer than six players from junior ranks have taken their places in representative or international games. One of them, W. Fullerton, is the reigning indoor British one mile skating title holder. Another, W. S. McLeod, besides playing Scotland at Hockey, played for his country in the golf internationals.

The premier Trophy in Scottish Ice-Hockey is the Mitchell Trophy, presented in 1929 by Andrew Mitchell, Esq., of Beechlands, Cathcart, Glasgow. Play is by knock out, and the winners to date are :—

1930.	Glasgow Skating Club.
1931.	Kelvingrove.
1932.	Queens.
1933.	Bears.
1934.	Kelvingrove.
1935.	Mohawks.
1936.	Mohawks.

The League winners since the inception of the Association are :—

Oct./Dec. 1919.	Bearsden.
Jan./Apl. 1930.	Mohawks, 1st Division ; Kelvingrove, 2nd Division.
1930/1931.	Kelvingrove (only one division since this year).
1931/1932.	Mohawks.
1932/1933.	Bridge of Weir.
1933/1934.	Kelvingrove.
1934/1935.	Bridge of Weir.
1935/1936.	Mohawks.

Since the season 1930–1931, the winners of the League have the custody of the Canada Cup, presented in 1930 by the Canada Cycle and Motor Co., of Weston, Ontario, Canada.

In 1933, Mr. Frank Stuart, President of the S.I.H.A., added further stimulus to the game by inaugurating a knock-out tournament, known as the President's Pucks, in which the members of the winning team each receive a silver-mounted puck. The first finalists in this tournament, Mohawks and Kelvingrove, played 110 minutes without either being able to inflict defeat on the other and, owing to the nearness of the close of the season, had to decide by the toss of a coin. The winners to date are :—

1933. Kelvingrove and Mohawks (no decision).
1934. Bridge of Weir.
1935. Mohawks.
1936. Mohawks.

Ice-Hockey in Scotland has received a further fillip this year with the building of a rink at Perth, to be opened in October. This rink has been constructed on lines very desirable to the spectator, in so much as the seating is by means of tiers of seats, every one of which gives an uninterrupted view of the rink. Great interest has been shown locally and a good beginning is anticipated. The rink will be known by the name Central Scotland Ice Rink, and the Manager is Mr. Adam Alexander.

INTERNATIONAL MATCH RESULTS

1909	Scotland	1	England	11	26 Mar.	Princes
1930	Gt. Britain	3	The Canadas	16	15 Mar.	Crossmyloof
1931	Scotland	9	North of England	0	16 Oct.	Liverpool
	Scotland	1	England	4	12 Dec.	Crossmyloof
1932	Scotland	1	English League	1	7 Jan.	Oxford
	Scotland	1	France	7	20 Oct.	Paris
	Scotland	1	Edmonton Superiors	8	26 Nov.	Crossmyloof
1933	Gt. Britain	0	Edmonton Superiors	7	28 Jan.	Crossmyloof
	Scotland	0	England	4	April	Oxford
	Scotland	0	North of England	0	18 Dec.	Crossmyloof
1934	Canada	5	U.S.A.	1	23 Jan.	Crossmyloof
1935	Gt. Britain	2	Winnipeg Monarchs	7	15 Mar.	Crossmyloof
	Scotland	3	England	6	16 Mar.	Wembley
1936	Scotland	1	England	1	14 Mar.	Crossmyloof

CHAPTER V

UNIVERSITY ICE-HOCKEY

1900

THE first Inter-'Varsity match was at Princes Skating Club on March 16th, 1900.

It was played under the title of

Mr. B. J. T. Bosanquet's Oxford team
v.
Mr. J. J. Cawthra's team.

OXFORD

B. J. T. Bosanquet (Oriel), Capt. ; E. C. Lee (University) ; J. G. Stevenson (New College) ; A. E. Severn (Christ Church) ; F. H. Latham (Trinity).

CAMBRIDGE

J. J. Cawthra (Clare), Capt. ; E. Northern (Trinity) ; G. C. Glenny (Pembroke) ; F. S. Kidd (Trinity) ; H. Banbury (Trinity).

Half-time scores :—
Oxford 6.   Cambridge 4.

Full-time scores :—
Oxford 7.   Cambridge 6.

OFFICIALS

Referee.—H. W. Page.

Goal Judges.—B. H. Hodson, J. G. Bishop, B. M. Patton, and J. K. L. Ross.

Oxford were insistent that the match should be played with bandy sticks or hockey sticks cut down to a similar length, also that a lacrosse ball should be used. " For the sake of peace and the fun of a game, we gave way to them," the Cambridge skipper wrote in the ' Log ' of the match.

The respective captains were the ' star ' players on each side, but J. J. Cawthra was much the better of the two, and of his own team stood out ' head and shoulders ' above all the others. If he had received better support he would have turned a very narrow defeat into a victory.

As this match is the first of the Inter-'Varsity matches it has been dealt with more fully than the limited space in the handbook will permit of being given to the remaining twenty-one matches.

Sketches of the very distinguished sports careers of the respective captains are also given.

Jack Cawthra, who lives in Toronto and was the founder of the Inter-'Varsity matches, was a very remarkable all-round athlete. He gained one Full Blue and two Half Blues : a Full Blue for Athletics and Half-Blues for Lacrosse and Speed-Skating.

At athletics he ran in the three miles for Cambridge v. Oxford in 1898–99–1900 ; in the half-mile against Oxford in 1901, and in this year also ran in the mile for Oxford and Cambridge v. Harvard and Yale in New York.

He was the Cambridge lacrosse captain 1899–1900, and played for England v. Canada in three International Matches which took place at Lord's, Oxford and Manchester.

At Ice-Hockey, in addition to being captain of Cambridge University, he played for England in the first International Ice-Hockey tournament ever organized at St. Moritz, which was for the Championship of the International Ice-Hockey League [1] in 1913.

At speed-skating he won the Cambridge University Races at Littleport in February 1901, while in figure-skating he was runner-up in the amateur Figure-Skating Championship of Canada at Ottawa in 1908. He is now a judge of figure-skating, and wrote the author that it was a *very cold job* standing on the ice for two long days in February

[1] In the Championship of the I.I.H.L., players other than ' Nationals ' could help the country they were residing in.

last officiating at the Canadian Amateur Figure-Skating Championships.

To have been a very distinguished Ice-Hockey player, speed-skater and figure-skater, also judge of the latter, is surely an absolutely unique ' Ice record.' J. J. Cawthra is also a very shrewd judge of the form of Ice-Hockey teams.

Bernard Bosanquet was a very distinguished cricketer, and played for Eton, Oxford, Middlesex and All England ; he was the famous ' Googly ' bowler.

On the evening following the 'Varsity match an Oxford and Cambridge team composed of

> J. J. Cawthra (Cambridge), (Capt.) ; B. J. Bosanquet, (Oxford) ; F. H. Latham (Oxford) ; G. C. Glenny (Cambridge), and J. G. Stevenson (Oxford)

beat Princes :—

> J. K. L. Ross, B. H. Hodson, H. B. Lindsay, C. I. Napier and B. M. Patton (Capt.)

by 7—2.

A ball was used for the first half of the game.

1901

At Princes on March 15th. Cambridge beat Oxford by 6 goals to 5.

OXFORD

> R. D. Hodson (University), goal ; A. Houghton (Merton), back ; A. C. Pawson (Christ Church) ; R. R. Smart (Pembroke) ; B. J. Bosanquet (Oriel), Capt.

CAMBRIDGE

> K. M. Chance (Trinity), goal ; C. M. G. Howell (Clare), back ; G. H. Dunn (Pembroke) ; J. H. Howell (Clare) ; J. J. Cawthra (Clare), Capt.

J. J. Cawthra 4 and J. H. Howell 2 goals scored for Cambridge. R. R. Smart 2, A. C. Pawson 2, and B. J. T. Bosanquet 1, scored for Oxford.

Referee.—H. W. Page.

Played with a rubber puck with bevelled edges and regulation hockey sticks.

On the succeeding evening, like last year, the combined 'Varsities met a Princes team, but this time the London team won 10—6.

OXFORD AND CAMBRIDGE

R. D. Hodson (Oxford), goal ; C. M. G. Howell (Cambridge), back ; R. R. Smart (Oxford) ; B. J. Bosanquet (Oxford) ; and J. J. Cawthra (Cambridge), Capt.

PRINCES

T. H. Curtis, goal ; B. H. Hodson, back ; J. S. Lindsay ; C. H. H. Hannaford ; and B. M. Patton, Capt.

Previous to the 'Varsity match on February 6th, Oxford met Princes and lost 13—4, but on March 6th in a return game the visitors only lost by the odd goal in fifteen.

1902

J. J. Cawthra endeavoured to arrange for the 'Varsity match to be played again this year. The Cantabs were invited to play a bandy match, *i.e.* with a ball, bandy stick and teams of eleven a side, on the lake at Blenheim Palace. The Cambridge captain agreed to this on the one condition that the Oxonians would play his 'Varsity at Ice-Hockey. To this they agreed but failed to do, giving as an excuse that they could not raise a team. The bandy match was played on February 18th; the result was a draw of 2 goals all.

Cambridge, who had a strong team this season, played three matches against Princes. On February 19th there was a drawn game of 9 all, but on March 15th they played Princes for the Admiral Maxe Cup and won 9—5. Their team was :—C. Duffield, goal ; C. M. G. Howell, back ; J. H. Howell ; G. Ogilvie ; and J. J. Cawthra, Capt.

In their third match against Princes, the Cantabs won 5—0.

In November an Oxford and Cambridge team drew with Princes.

1903

On January 31st, Cambridge drew with Princes 7—7, but on March 14th lost the Challenge Cup to London Club by the narrow margin of 2 goals to the home side's 3.

On November 7th Cambridge joined the first Ice-Hockey League ever formed in England, but Oxford did not.

Cambridge came out fifth (last place).

Played 8. Won 1. Drawn 0. Lost 7.

1906

It was not until this year that either 'Varsity again took part in Ice-Hockey. Rhodes scholars at Oxford formed a team and called themselves Oxford Canadians, and in March played two games against Princes, the second of which they won.

On December 5th and 12th they met the London team again, but lost on both occasions.

1907

Two matches were played by the Oxford Canadians against Princes on December 3rd and 11th respectively. The first they lost 8—1, but the second they won 8—4 ; the home team on the latter occasion was very weakly represented. The Canadians, however, on March 10th won the Princes Challenge Cup, and their names were :—R. V. Bellamy ; H. M. Bond ; S. M. Herbert ; J. M. Macdonnell ; R. C. Reade ; and G. S. Stairs, Capt.

1908

On February 19th, Princes beat the Oxford men 10—2, and on March 17th by 7—2 ; the latter, a drawn game of seven goals each, was played between these teams on December 2nd.

1909

Only one match was recorded as having been played by the Oxford Canadians ; this was on March 16th. The result

is not known, but it was not for the cup as the Princes
team was unchallenged for it this year.

Sir Henry Lunn revived the Inter-'Varsity match this
year. It was played at Wengen in Switzerland on December
2nd. Oxford won 5—3.

There were no Rhodes scholars playing for Oxford
although the form of Meigs might possibly have been considered as worthy of one, had the participants in the
matches have heard of the repute of the men from overseas.

As this ' historic ' match may make rather interesting
reading, a correct and unblemished account is given despite
some slight and recent amendments !

This was the first match for the Challenge Cup presented
by the Alpine Sports Club, and took place at the early
hour of 10.30 a.m. Originally it was intended to be a
three-days' contest but a thaw set in. The match was
postponed until the latest possible date, and in consequence
only one game was played. The ice was very soft as the
result of the thaw, and the man in charge of the ice had
made it far worse than it even should have been by flooding
it early in the morning.

There had been a discussion between the sides as to
whether bandy or hockey sticks should be used. Cambridge
wanted the former and Oxford the latter. Bandy sticks
were used, and Oxford was further handicapped by her
team having practised with a puck and consequently over-
skating the wooden block used at the request of Cambridge.
The match was a very scratch affair, and the Oxford goalie
provided the chief interest. On land he was no doubt a
fine hockey player, but unfortunately he could not skate,
so he played goal, where he saved his charge by throwing
himself across the path of the ' palet,' thus anticipating a
rule which did not come into force until some eighteen
years later ! All went well with him until half-time, when
he had to change ends, and it was only with the support
of the two backs and the cheers of the spectators that he
was enabled to cross the rink ! Half-time score was 3—2
in favour of Cambridge, who hitherto seem to have had
everything their own way—sticks, ' palet ' and a lead of
one goal ! Someone on the Oxford side seems at that

period to have had a ' brain-wave ' ! Meigs, apparently
their ' star,' was moved up into the forward line, and he
got two more goals in addition to the one he had got in
the first half. Oxford thus led by the odd goal in seven,
and just before time Spread got another, so the ' Dark
Blues ' won a remarkable match by 5—3. The game was
an even one and fairly represented the ' merits ' of the
two teams. Watson averted many disasters : his timely
falls to save despite that on occasions his opponents swept
him away complete with goal. Mention should be made of
the other goal scorers in this historic match in addition to
Meigs. They were Spread and Winter for Oxford, but
unfortunately the historians forgot to record who supplied
the Cantabs' quota. It will be noticed that there were
eight in each team and hence two cover points.

OXFORD

P. Watson (Merton), goal ; R. A. Arderne (Merton)
point ; T. L. Forbes (University), cover point ; D. R.
Meigs (Merton), cover point ; F. E. Hawkins, Capt.
(University), rover ; H. K. Lunn (New College), H. A.
Winter (University), E. R. Spread (Exeter), forwards.

CAMBRIDGE

C. T. Swift (King's), goal ; H. C. and F. G. Hudson
(Jesus), point and cover point ; P. R. May (Pembroke),
rover ; D. R. J. Holliday, cover point ; M. E. C. and
R. Baggalay (Trinity) and A. W. M. S. Griffin, Capt.
(Trinity), forwards.

Rev. G. A. Scott (Emmanuel) was also present, but perhaps
as spare man. Positions approximately correct.

Referee.—C. Perowne.

Each member of the winning team received a small gold
hockey stick.

1910

This year the Oxford Canadians visited Switzerland and
played *hors concours* in the European Championship at Les
Avants, which took place January 10th–12th. Bad

weather caused the abandonment of the matches the day before they were scheduled to end. Ice conditions were extremely bad all the three days. The idea in letting the Rhodes scholars take part in the tournament was to enable the spectators to get an idea as to their style of play. In the event of their winning, they could not, of course, not being a European team, claim the title of European champions. In their first match the Oxford team beat Switzerland 8—1 and then proceeded to beat Germany and Belgium also. They did not meet the English team owing to a sudden decision to change the time of the game. This change is referred to in the account of the European Championship elsewhere.

A match on November 26 between the Oxford Canadians and Princes was an even one, the former winning 7—5.

OXFORD *v.* CAMBRIDGE

Played at Mürren in December 1910.

Oxford won 5—3 after ten minutes over time. The play in this match, like its predecessor, was again of a very low standard, a shade better is about the best that can be said of it. No Rhodes scholars took part or it would have been the massacre of Cambridge, of course. Falls were very frequent due to insufficient skating ability ; these were not to be wondered at because in those days there was neither indoor nor outdoor ice. There were no attendants with sponges, towels, oranges, etc., officially arranged for ! There was, however, a certain ' Official ' who was known as the ' Refresheree,' and who, to a certain extent, anticipated the present-day attendants to teams. When there were intervals between periods of practice each afternoon, this ' Official ' would sally forth from the adjoining restaurant with greatly appreciated refreshments, not necessarily of the teetotal kind ! It is not improbable that he did the same during the actual match, which would also partly account for the numerous falls !

Oxford Captain.—P. Watson.

Cambridge Captain.—The Lord Carberry.

Referee.—E. T. Whitehead.

1911

Oxford Canadians took part in International Tournaments at Les Avants and Chamonix in January, where they inflicted heavy defeats on the Princes team, which was depleted through injuries to several players, by 12—0 and 12—1.

OXFORD v. CAMBRIDGE

At Mürren, December 22nd, 1911.

Cambridge won 2—0. Both goals were scored early in the first half. The Oxford captain and G. Riviers, two of the best players, had not been on skates previous to the match.

Oxford Captain.—The Lord St. Leonards.
Cambridge Captain.—The Lord Carberry.

1912

OXFORD v. CAMBRIDGE

At Mürren, December 23rd.

Cambridge won 1—0, scored by P. Barrow just before ' Time.' Play was of a much higher standard than in the three preceding 'Varsity matches.

Oxford Captain.—The Lord St. Leonards.
Cambridge Captain.—F. A. Phillipps.
Referee.—B. M. Patton.

1913

OXFORD v. CAMBRIDGE

At Mürren, December 23rd.

Cambridge 10, Oxford 0. The result of this match did not of course indicate the true strength of the two 'Varsities. Had Oxford been allowed to play their Rhodes scholars, the score might have been just the reverse. The idea in excluding Rhodes scholars was to ensure an even game between the English players of both Universities.

A vague rule as to their exclusion existed, but after the

match it was to a certain extent rescinded, and in the
future two players from North America could be included
in each team. Vetter, who was easily the best man on
either team, had learned his hockey at Princes, scored
5 goals and Ayre 3. Wenham in goal had only one shot to
deal with.

Cambridge Captain.—F. A. Phillipps (Trinity).
Oxford Captain.—R. G. Cassten (Hertford).
Referee.—B. M. Patton.

1920

OXFORD *v.* CAMBRIDGE

At Mürren in December.

Cambridge o, Oxford o, after five minutes each way of
extra time, previous to which three periods of ten minutes
each had been played, instead of the usual two of twenty
minutes each.

The standard of play was a good deal higher than in any
previous 'Varsity matches, due to the presence of Canadian
players in both teams. The most prominent of these was
Ken Taylor, the first of a line of fine captains and distinguished players that it has been Oxford's lot to have. It
was the splendid work of Taylor in goal that saved his
side from defeat, for Cambridge were undoubtedly the
stronger team. At the end of the second period, a novelty
for those days occurred ; the ice was scraped and swept, a
vital necessity, for the sun was in very good form that
morning.

Oxford Captain.—K. E. Taylor (probably).
Cambridge Captain.—A. R. C. Adamson (Magdalene).
Referee.—B. M. Patton.

1921

On January 8th and 9th K. E. Taylor, Oxford, A. C. N.
Gosling and A. R. C. Adamson, Cambridge, assisted England
to win the Bouvier Cup at St. Moritz.

1921–22

On October 23rd, 1921, in Ken Taylor's rooms at Oriel, the Oxford University Ice-Hockey Club was formed and the following officials were elected :—

K. E. Taylor.	*Captain.*	Oriel.
F. L. L. Neylan.	*Hon. Secretary.*	Pembroke.
C. B. Gull, M.A.	*Hon. Treasurer.*	St. Edmund's Hall.
E. B. Pitblado.	*Jun. Treasurer.*	Queen's.

CAMBRIDGE

A. R. C. Adamson.   *Captain.*   Magdalene.

On November 9th, 1921, at a meeting of the club it was decided that it should be affiliated to the B.I.H.A.

Prior to going to Switzerland, Taylor, who took his duties very seriously, brought two teams to Manchester for a trial game. Then with the other officials he organized the first of Oxford's continental tours, which began at Antwerp with a 5—1 victory over that club.

OXFORD *v.* CAMBRIDGE

At Mürren, December 22nd, 1921.

Oxford 27, Cambridge 0. The overwhelming defeat of Cambridge was due chiefly to Oxford being represented by one of the finest, if not the finest, team that that University has ever had. If the Cambridge captain, in marked contrast to the Oxford one, had taken as much trouble as Taylor had in getting a team together and giving it some practice, the match might perhaps not have been such a very mediocre one. The form of the Oxford men was so well known that a sweepstake was got up before the match as to how many goals they would get. The man who drew forty goals refused to sell his chance after the first five minutes !

Referee.—B. M. Patton.

The Oxford team made history. It never came anywhere near being defeated although it met the strongest teams in Europe.

After the 'Varsity match Oxford defeated the Swiss National team 9—0, with subsequent and bigger victories over Davos and St. Moritz at those resorts.

On the tour they amassed in all eighty-seven goals to the two of their opponents !

To Taylor can be given chief credit for inaugurating three wonderful seasons of Oxford, 1921–22, 1922–23, and 1923-24, Hockey. It can be called the Taylor-Pitblado-Bonnycastle era, for these were the chief ' stars ' in the teams of those three seasons. R. H. Bonnycastle, the first of the three celebrated brothers who represented Oxford, was a member of the 1921–22 team. Taylor, however, was only at Oxford for the first two seasons of this era.

Five Oxford players, for whom special leave had been obtained, returned to St. Moritz in February to assist the English team in an International Tournament. It was entirely owing to their help that the British team won, for unless their help had been available a British team could not have been got together. Those who came were E. B. Pitblado, H. Fleming, F. L. Neylan, F. M. Bacon and C. B. Clark. The very plucky act of Fleming is well worth recording. In the first match he nearly bit his tongue right through, but after getting it stitched he played in the other matches. Without his help it is very doubtful whether we should have been successful.

1922–23

Officers

OXFORD

K. E. Taylor.	*Captain.*	Oriel.
L. B. Pearson.	*Hon. Secretary.*	Queen's.
C. B. Gull, M.A.	*Hon. Sen. Treasurer.*	St. Edmund's Hall.
E. B. Pitblado.	*Hon. Jun. Secretary.*	Queen's.

CAMBRIDGE

H. G. Joseph.	*Captain.*	Trinity.

OXFORD v. CAMBRIDGE

At Mürren, December 25th.

Oxford 7, Cambridge 1. This was a far better game than any previous one between the 'Varsities. The Cambridge captain had displayed great energy and taken a great deal of trouble to find the best available material. He was perhaps lucky in getting a team together of which nearly all the members had played in Canada or the U.S.A. He also provided adequate training. He was perhaps unlucky in being opposed to another wonderful Oxford side.

For the first time three periods of twenty minutes each were played.

Referee.—Col. H. Molson.

Some of Oxford's other victories in this their second and very successful tour were over the German National team in Berlin, Paris, Davos and the British Army at St. Moritz. The match with the soldiers was played very shortly after their arrival from England ; they were all Canadians and gave the Oxford men a bit of a shock. At the end of the first fifteen minutes the Army led 3—2, but at the end of the second period it was 5—5, then lack of training and the altitude began to tell and Oxford won 10—5.

The Cambridge captain also organized a tour this winter but not so ambitious as the Oxford one ; nevertheless it was successful. Two of their wins were over Davos and the British Army.

For the first time Oxford sent a second team to the Continent, as also did Cambridge. They were called ' A ' teams and met at Davos ; the Oxonians won a fairly even game, 5—2.

1923–24

Officers

OXFORD

E. B. Pitblado.	*Captain.*	Queen's.
R. H. G. Bonnycastle.	*Hon. Secretary.*	Wadham.
C. B. Gull, M.A.	*Hon. Sen. Treasurer.*	St. Edmund's Hall.
E. A. Manton.	*Jun. Treasurer.*	

CAMBRIDGE

W. H. Anderson. *Captain.* Caius.

OXFORD *v.* CAMBRIDGE

At Mürren, December 29th, 1923.

Oxford 3, Cambridge 0. Heavy snow which fell throughout the match rendered good hockey out of the question. Oxford had the stronger team, and under normal conditions would have won by a larger margin.

Oxford and Cambridge again made continental tours, and both played matches against the British Olympic team. Except that Oxford again had an extraordinarily successful tour, no actual results are to hand.

1924–25

Officers

J. W. Sears.	*Captain.*	Merton.	Cambridge.
D. M. Johnson.	*Hon. Secretary.*	Balliol.	Captain.
C. B. Gull, M.A.	*Hon. Sen. Treasurer.*	St. Edmund's Hall.	
W. Hurst Brown.	*Jun. Treasurer.*	Queen's.	

There was no 'Varsity match this season. The Oxford Committee was in favour of its being played again at Mürren, but for some reason arrangements for it to be so could not be made. Both the Oxford and Cambridge teams during their respective tours were at St. Moritz at the same time in January. The writer was asked to negotiate with them for the 'Varsity match to be played there. Cambridge were willing to play on the terms offered them by the hotels, but Oxford would not agree to them and so the match fell through. This was a pity, for, judging by the results of the games that both teams had played against the same teams, they were extremely well matched. Cambridge, the results of whose tour previous to St. Moritz are not to hand, beat St. Moritz 2—1 and London Lions 2—0. The latter match was a re-play after the previous afternoon, for the reason that ten minutes before

time, when the Lions were leading 2—1, a sudden gale
blew down and away the high boards behind one of the
goals, together with the goal and the writer, who was in it,
complete ! Oxford lost to the Lions 4—3 after five minutes
over time, but beat St. Moritz 3—1.

Oxford also sent an ' A ' team to Switzerland under the
captaincy of Neville Melland (Trinity), who eventually
became one of England's captains and best-known players.
He has also distinguished himself very much at lacrosse.

Results of Oxford's first team matches :—

Played 14. Won 9. Drawn 2. Lost 3.

Davos Cup won.

1925–26

Officers

OXFORD

H. Borden.	*Captain.*	Exeter.
G. White.	*Hon. Secretary.*	Keble.
F. N. S. Melland.	*Hon. Treasurer.*	Trinity.

CAMBRIDGE

| E. H. Quainton. | *Captain.* | Queens'. |

OXFORD *v.* CAMBRIDGE

At St. Moritz, January 4th, 1926.

Oxford 11, Cambridge 0.   The Dark Blues won by a
larger margin than might have been anticipated because
the matches between them and the Lions and the Lions
and Cambridge were all very even.   The second Bonnycastle brother played in this match, but his form did not
quite equal that of his elder brother or Larry, who came to
Oxford about four years later.

As the last 'Varsity match was played in 1923 and the
next in 1926, it would appear that there had been an
interval of three years between them.   Such, however, is
not really the case, because from December 29th, 1923, to
January 4th, 1926, is only six days more than two years
so three matches could not have been played in that period.

There are no available match records of the teams previous to their visit to St. Moritz, where Oxford drew one game with and lost one to the London Lions 3—2 but beat St. Moritz 5—2. Cambridge lost twice to the Lions by small margins.

Earl Thoenan (Exeter) proved a very able business manager to the Oxford team.

1926–27

Officers

OXFORD

G. White.	*Captain.*	Keble.
D. H. Moore.	*Hon. Secretary.*	St. Catherine's.
A. Wallace Johnson.	*Hon. Treasurer.*	Brasenose.

CAMBRIDGE

F. Murray Forbes.	*Captain.*	Caius.
Durrand Smith.	*Hon. Secretary.*	Caius.

Oxford toured as usual, but there is no record of their achievements.

Clarence Campbell played for England against the Montreal Victorias at the Ice Club on March 9th.

Amongst other matters decided upon at the meeting of February 7th, when the above officers for the ensuing season were elected, was the decision to have a photo taken of the team. It was arranged to have it taken at a certain shop, " but some impecunious ones," it is recorded, " protested for some cheaper shop where they were not so well known " !

OXFORD *v.* CAMBRIDGE

At St. Moritz, January 6th, 1927.

Cambridge 3, Oxford 0. The first time Cambridge had won since 1913.

Cambridge, in F. Murray Forbes, had a captain to whom great credit is due for the keenness and energy he applied to his work. One very important thing he had done was to have a detailed record kept of his team's tour; a precedent that has been followed ever since. He played for England *v.* Belgium on April 2nd.

Exclusive of Spengler Cup matches, in which the semi-finals were reached, the Cambridge record was :—

Tour and 'Varsity.

Played	Won	Drawn	Lost	Goals for	Goals against
12	9	0	3	36	32

1927–28

Officers

OXFORD

C. S. Campbell.	*Captain.*	Lincoln.
A. D. Stoddard.	*Hon. Secretary.*	Trinity.
H. A. Allard.	*Hon. Treasurer.*	St. John's.

CAMBRIDGE

A. S. Whiting.	*Captain.*
E. B. McKee.	*Hon. Secretary.*

OXFORD *v.* CAMBRIDGE

At St. Moritz, January 7th, 1928.
Cambridge 1, Oxford 0.

Referee.—R. Bell (Member of the Montreal Victorias, first Canadian team to play in England).

A very even game and noticeable for the great work of Campbell, who stood out head and shoulders above the rest of the team. C. W. Wylde on defence and W. G. Speechley in goal did best for Cambridge, for whom F. H. de Marwicz shot the only goal of the match. The first two players named were members of the British Olympic team of this year, on which de Marwicz was also invited to play but could not get leave from Cambridge.

There is no record of the tours of either Oxford's first or second team ; G. Lead was captain of the latter.

CAMBRIDGE MATCH RECORD

Tour and 'Varsity.

Played	Won	Drawn	Lost	Goals for	Goals against
16	8	2	6	34	31

1928–29

Officers

OXFORD

C. S. Campbell.	*Captain.*	Lincoln.
B. P. Davis.	*Hon. Secretary.*	Magdalen.
P. K. Hennessy.	*Treasurer.*	Brasenose.

CAMBRIDGE

C. T. Wylde.	*Captain.*	Caius.
The Earl of Lincoln.	*Hon. Secretary.*	Magdalene.

OXFORD *v.* CAMBRIDGE

At St. Moritz, January 6th, 1929.

Oxford 1, Cambridge 0. It was a very fitting reward for Clarence Campbell that his team should win the 'Varsity match, though by such a small margin. Clarence Campbell was one of the very finest captains that Oxford ever had. As an appreciation of the great services that he had rendered the club during the past two years, the members presented him with a suitably engraved miniature of the Anspang Cup. A committee of two was appointed to present him also with a miniature of the Patton Cup. R. Bush, who scored Oxford's goal, was given a miniature of the latter cup as well as his captain.

Oxford had a very successful tour, during which the Anspang Cup was won for the third time in succession.

The Cambridge tour was also very successful.

Tour and 'Varsity.

Played	Won	Drawn	Lost	Goals for	Goals against
13	.11	1	1	39	16

Berlin, by 1 goal to 0, was the only team that beat Cambridge. This was in the final for the Spengler Cup after three periods of overtime play.

1929-30

Officers

OXFORD

D. M. Turnbull.	*Captain.*	St. John's.
A. J. Grace.	*Hon. Secretary.*	St. John's.
R. Maitland.	*Hon. Treasurer.*	Hertford.

CAMBRIDGE

W. G. Speechley.	*Captain.*	St. John's.
F. A. de Marwicz.	*Hon. Secretary.*	Pembroke.

OXFORD *v.* CAMBRIDGE

At St. Moritz, January 8th, 1930.
Cambridge 2, Oxford 1. A drawn game, however, would have represented the actual play better.

Oxford Tour.

Played	Won	Drawn	Lost	Goals for	Goals against
14	5	1	8	39	44

Cambridge Tour.

Played	Won	Drawn	Lost	Goals for	Goals against
19	10	4	5	38	26

During their tour Oxford won the Anspang Cup, a cup for competition between the 'Varsity and Davos only, for the fourth time, which entitled her to keep it. At a general meeting of the club in May it was agreed to offer . the cup for competition again between the two clubs.

On February 13th, the combined 'Varsity teams, W. G. Speechley (Captain), met the visiting Canadian team, the Canadas, at Golders Green rink and were defeated 13—0.

1930–31

Officers

OXFORD

R. Martland.	*Captain.*	Hertford.
L. C. Bonnycastle.	*Hon. Secretary.*	Wadham.
J. D. Babbitt.	*Hon. Treasurer.*	University.

CAMBRIDGE

Baron H. Von Trauttenberg.	*Captain.*	Pembroke.
F. A. de Marwicz.	(Co-opted).	Pembroke.
J. H. Fawcett.	*Hon. Secretary.*	Clare.

OXFORD *v.* CAMBRIDGE

At St. Moritz, January 6th, 1931.
Oxford 5, Cambridge 1.
    Referee.—D. Trovati, Milan I.H.C.

OXFORD MATCH RECORD

All Matches.
    Played 21.   Won 15.   Drawn 2.   Lost 4.

The newly opened rink at Oxford had proved of great assistance in building up a team. With the appearance of Larry Bonnycastle, the third brother to assist the Dark Blues, another great era in Oxford hockey began. L. C. Bonnycastle made the first of a number of appearances for England in the match against the Manitoba Grads in March. The 'Varsity met the Grads and put up a good game against them, only losing by 4—0. This season Oxford had one of its greatest teams of recent years. To compare it with those great unbeaten teams of 1921–22–23 is difficult. No doubt R. H. and L. C. Bonnycastle could argue long about it, if they have not already done so. Those earlier teams were better balanced and had no spare forwards as weak as Oxford's second line this season. The Pitblado-Bonnycastle combination was about the equal of the Babbitt-Bonnycastle one ; very little difference between the goalkeepers, if any, but the 1931–32 defence may have been the least shade stronger.

H. C. Little, Oxford's great goalkeeper, played for England at Krynica in the European and World Championships.

CAMBRIDGE MATCH RECORD

All Matches.

Played	Won	Drawn	Lost	Goals for	Goals against
14	10	0	4	32	18

In addition to being captain of Cambridge, Dicky Trauttenberg was captain of the Austrian team, for the first time, which won the European Championship at Krynica in Poland.

B. H. Fawcett, A. MacCullum and F. A. de Marwicz of this year's Cambridge team also played for England during this season, as did P. M. Churchill a year or two afterwards.

1931–32

Officers

OXFORD

L. C. Bonnycastle.	*President and Captain.*	Wadham.
C. H. Little.	*Hon. Secretary.*	Brasenose.
J. D. Babbitt.	*Hon. Treasurer.*	University.

CAMBRIDGE

| P. M. Churchill. | *Captain.* | Caius. |
| J. B. Morgan. | *Hon. Secretary.* | Trinity. |

OXFORD *v.* CAMBRIDGE

At Richmond, February 6th, 1932.

Oxford 7, Cambridge 0. Not since 1901 had the 'Varsity match been played in England. It was a pity that the ' Full House ' did not witness a more even game. This season Oxford was represented by one of the finest teams ever, whilst that of Cambridge was a mere shadow of last season's. The former had few good players left, whereas the Cambridge captain and secretary were the only two who played the previous year.

Taking this into consideration, and the big handicap with the long journeys to London to practise, Peter Churchill must be credited with having displayed great keenness and done all he could to make a brave show against great odds. Cambridge acted mainly on the defensive and relied on individual or two-men rushes, which did not get them far against the powerful ' Bonny-Babbitt ' combination, plus an equally powerful defence behind which was the best goalkeeper in the country at that time. The Oxford scribe's account of the game was mostly in light vein. Referring to the one called S . . . ks, who was penalised, his effort was thus : " I saw him make attempts on more than one occasion before his penalty laid his ' Tab ' low on the icy field, not good enough ! This method of pursuing an adversary with now a shove and then a shove until he finally drops for the count is typical of keen skating instinct, but alas ! too liable to catch the eye of his Nibs the referee."

His NIBS in this match was England's captain, J. C. P. Magwood.

OXFORD MATCH RECORD

	Played	Won	Drawn	Lost	Goals for	Goals against
Tour .	14	9	2	3	38	10
Other Matches	5	2	2	1	14	9
League .	12	12	0	0	54	8
Total .	31	23	4	4	106	27

'Varsity match counts as four points, as the teams can only meet once a year.

Oxford won three cups this season, the Anspang, the Spengler and the Patton (latter for League Championship).

For the first time a record was kept of goals and ' assists.' One of the best matches of the season was

against the Boston Olympics, which was a draw. The
same Oxford forward line played the whole game ! The
Bostonians had previously beaten England and France.

Herbie Little described Queen's Rink as being like a
Bowling Alley. If he had seen the old Princes, one which
was the same length as Queen's but only 52 ft. wide, he
might have called that a Shooting Gallery.

The Oxford team was presented with gold medals by the
Mayor of the town as a token of appreciation and as a
memento of an unbeaten League record. The Oxford
scribe wrote of the event that ' Bonny's ' speeches were
not so good as his goals and advised him to take up pro.
hockey instead of the Bar as a career !

CAMBRIDGE MATCH RECORD

All Matches.

Played	Won	Drawn	Lost	Goals for	Goals against
14	0	0	14	14	81

1932–1933

Officers

OXFORD

C. H. Little.	*Captain.*	Brasenose.
J. E. Coyne.	*Hon. Secretary.*	Queen's.
A. S. Leach.	*Hon. Treasurer.*	University.

CAMBRIDGE

D. C. Gattiker.	*Captain.*
J. T. Cahan.	*Hon. Secretary.*

J. T. Cahan was unfortunately killed in a motor accident
in December 1932 and the vacancy not filled.

For Oxford hockey the most important event of the
season was the award of ' Half-Blues.'

OXFORD v. CAMBRIDGE

At Oxford, January 21st, 1933.

Oxford 1, Cambridge 0. A far more even game than

was anticipated. Not until five minutes before the end did Johnson get the only goal obtained as the result of an ' assist ' by Babbitt. Douglas in the Cambridge goal was to a very great extent responsible for Oxford being held for so long ; he had no chance of saving Johnson's shot.

Referee.—J. C. P. Magwood.

The following players represented Oxford in the 'Varsity match, and in consequence were the recipients of the Half-Blues awarded for Ice-Hockey.

C. H. Little (Toronto and Brasenose), Capt. ; A. S. Leach (Dartmouth and University), O. A. Gratias (Saskatchewan and Brasenose), G. H. Johnson (McGill and Wadham), L. A. Watson (Minnesota and Hertford), J. D. Babbitt (New Brunswick and University), A.] H. Humble (New Brunswick and Worcester), S. R. Hopkins (Saskatchewan and Queen's), E. A. McCourt (Alberta and Merton).

J. E. Coyne (Manitoba and Queen's) was selected to play, but he unluckily got influenza on the day of the match and so was prevented from being one of the first group of Ice-Hockey Blues.

OXFORD MATCH RECORD

	Played	Won	Drawn	Lost	Goals for	Goals against
Tour .	14	5	3	6	13	12
English League .	8	8	0	0	35	3
Other Matches .	5	1	2	2	3	5
Total	27	14	5	8	51	20

Oxford made about the most arduous tour this winter that was ever undertaken by probably any Ice-Hockey team, and the Oxford scribe wrote " that it would probably constitute a record both in geographical variety and distance travelled. Aeroplane, railway, steam-boat, train-ferry, motor-coach, taxis, one open horse-sleigh and to-boggans, in addition to 'Shanks' Pony,' were the chief modes of travel employed ; dog-sleighs, bath chairs and rickshaws were about the only vehicles that the team did not have recourse to."

Oxford lost the Anspang Cup, shared the Spengler and Hanseatic Cups with Prague, but again won the Patton Cup (English League Championship).

CAMBRIDGE MATCH RECORD

	Played	Won	Drawn	Lost	Goals for	Goals against
Tour	. 16	0	1	15	13	70
English League	. 1	0	0	1	0	1
Other Matches	. 8	3	1	4	18	43
Cambridge Eskimos	. 14	3	1	10	24	52

R. D. Douglas was captain of the Cambridge Eskimos and D. C. G. Gattiker (Cambridge) has played for England.

G. H. Johnson (Oxford), who now plays for Manchester, has played several times for England.

1933–34

Officers

OXFORD

J. E. Coyne	*President and Captain.*	Queen's.
E. R. Hopkins.	*Hon. Secretary.*	Wadham.
G. H. Johnson.	*Treasurer.*	Queen's.
J. D. Babbitt.	*Adviser.*	University.

CAMBRIDGE

R. T. L. Rogers.	*Captain.*	Downing.
R. F. Douglas.	*Hon. Secretary.*	Christ's.

Oxford v. Cambridge

At Oxford, January 20th, 1934.

Oxford 4, Cambridge 2.—The Oxford captain got over his initial difficulty of building up a team out of ten forwards with considerable success. He was lucky in having five ' Old Blues ' in addition to himself ; a very good nucleus to start from compared with only three ' old hands ' that Rogers took over.

In J. E. Nadeau, Coyne had one excellent new player, and in ' Jimmy ' Carr, ' Bob ' Rogers had an exceptionally good ' recruit ' from the R.M.C., Canada. It was owing to the fine work of the two last-named players that Cambridge put up such a good show against a better-balanced team. It was hard luck, however, for the Light Blues, as well as for himself, that R. F. Douglas their goalkeeper was unable to play owing to an injury. Oxford still had a rink but the Cambridge home rink was at Purley—a long journey. In making these long journeys to and from practice, the Light Blues displayed great keenness and a very sporting spirit.

Referees.—A. G. Duncanson and F. A. de Marwicz.

The Oxford tour has been described as ' the High-water Mark ' of the season from enjoyment, interest and hockey success, and not the least from the fact that it was for the first time financially self-supporting. The reason for this pleasing statement is no doubt due to the work of S. R. Hopkins, an Hon. Sec. never previously surpassed for efficiency in the annals of Oxford Ice-Hockey history, combined with an extremely competent business manager, C. S. Cowan. While in Berlin the team was greatly pleased at meeting the courteous and charming German Sports Minister, Herr von Tschammer und Osten. Many of us who were at the recent Winter Olympic Games also had the great pleasure of meeting this gentleman.

Referring to League matches, the Oxford scribe wrote :— " It was the first time we had met so much Canadian talent as the Grosvenor House Canadians and Queen's teams. We had a very difficult row to hoe and, though third in the league, gave all the clubs something to think about."

Match Summary

OXFORD

	Played	Won	Drawn	Lost	Goals for	Goals against
Tour .	20	9	1	11	31	15
English League .	12	7	1	4	58	23
Exhibition Matches .	4	1	0	3	5	17
Total	36	17	2	18	94	55

The Oxford Hon. Sec. wrote a most excellent, comprehensible and well-worded report of the season's doings.

CAMBRIDGE

	Played	Won	Drawn	Lost	Goals for	Goals against
Tour .	12	3	1	8	33	51
English League .	8	0	0	8	4	32

H. R. U. Greenwood managed the team on tour.

Owing to lack of support from the University authorities, the team was unable to complete its League fixtures.

The Eskimos, under the captaincy of D. G. C. Gattiker, also made a tour, but their record is incomplete.

R. T. Rogers and J. Carr played for England on a number of occasions.

1934–1935

Officers

OXFORD

E. Russell Hopkins.	*President.*	Queen's.
G. C. Andrew.	*Hon. Secretary.*	Balliol.
R. W. Black.	*Treasurer.*	
J. D. Babbitt.	*Executive.*	University.
G. S. Cowan.	{ *Business and* } { *General Manager.* }	Exeter.

CAMBRIDGE

| J. C. Carr. | *Captain.* | King's. |
| A. S. Tanner. | *Hon. Secretary* | Jesus. |

Owing to the Oxford rink having closed down at the end of the last season, and an offer from Hammersmith not being accepted, it was decided to withdraw from the League until such time as suitable accommodation could be found. Richmond made an offer later and Oxford accepted it.

Cambridge had to drop out of the League as no home rink was available. Two practices at Richmond and one at Wembley were all that the Light Blues had before their tour, and on their return they had one just before the 'Varsity match at Richmond.

OXFORD v. CAMBRIDGE

At Richmond, January 22nd, 1935.

Oxford 3, Cambridge 2. It was anticipated that Oxford, with the advantages of a home rink plus plenty of League games, would win. Cambridge, however, as on previous occasions were at a disadvantage but made a great effort and only lost by the odd goal in five. If Cambridge had possessed another player as good as ' Jimmy ' Carr, the Dark Blues would probably have had to be content with a draw or even possibly have been defeated.

Referees.—Major W. H. Mackenzie and G. Shouldis.

OXFORD MATCH RECORD

	Played	Won	Drawn	Lost	Goals for	Goals against
Tour	15	9	1	5	46	23
English League and 'Varsity	13	3	2	8	24	47
Total.	28	12	3	13	70	70

Oxford's second match against the Richmond Hawks

was in some respects the best of the season. Owing to Hopkins' superb exhibition in goal the 'Varsity only lost 2—1 to such extremely formidable opponents.

J. D. Babbitt, who did not play in the 'Varsity match, established a record. This made his sixth season in the Oxford team, as he went up in the summer term of 1930 ! He gave more ' assists ' this season than any other player, though only getting six goals.

E. R. Hopkins rendered Oxford U.I.H.C. very exceptional services in his capacities first as Hon. Secretary and then as President and Captain, apart from his very fine work in goal. One marked service was to form an executive committee of four members besides himself and draw up Rules of Constitution. These simple and practical rules, seventeen in all with a few sub-sections, included three with two sub-sections which applied specially to the Oxford Cosmopolitans.

At the annual general meeting of the club in March 1935, the Rules of Constitution were incorporated into the minutes of the O.U.I.H.C.

After the meeting there was a dinner, at which a presentation was made to E. R. Hopkins and a vote of thanks given for his very efficient management of the affairs of the club during the past season.

CAMBRIDGE MATCH RECORD

	Played	Won	Drawn	Lost	Goals for	Goals against
1st Team Tour .	15	7	0	8	45	60
Eskimos Tour .	7	1	2	4	17	24

J. C. Carr scored twenty-five goals and gave seven 'assists'; what would Cambridge have done without him ? Besides him only one player, C. E. Wark, showed any ability to score, and no doubt a good many of his eleven goals were the results of ' assists ' from his captain.

F. W. Finnigan (Trinity) was captain of the Eskimos.

1935–36
Officers
OXFORD

G. S. Cowan.	{President and Captain of team.}	Exeter.
C. C. Eberts.	*Hon. Secretary.*	Trinity.
R. L. Fenerty.	*Hon. Treasurer.*	University.

CAMBRIDGE

P. E. Holmes.	*Captain.*	Jesus.
F. S. Tanner.	*Hon. Secretary.*	Jesus.

OXFORD *v.* CAMBRIDGE

At Earl's Court, February 10th, 1936.
Referee.—F. A. de Marwicz.

Cambridge 2, Oxford 0. A Light Blue victory had been anticipated, but if G. S. Cowan had had another player of his standard to help him the result might have been a draw. Earl's Court was the home rink of both teams, so it was a fitting venue for the match.

OXFORD MATCH RECORD

	Played	Won	Drawn	Lost
Tour	21	5	3	13
League Matches	7	0	0	7
Other Matches	2	1	0	1
Total	30	6	3	21

CAMBRIDGE MATCH RECORD

	Played	Won	Drawn	Lost	Goals for	Goals against
English Matches including 'Varsity	5	1	0	4	11	49
Tour	14	8	2	4	55	43

In two of the English matches thirty-four goals were scored! Birmingham won 17—1, and Manchester 10—6. Double-figure scores were reached by Birmingham in that club's other two games with Cambridge.

RESULTS OF INTER-'VARSITY MATCHES

Oxford won 13.   Goal score, 92
Cambridge won 8.   Goal score, 45.
One match drawn.

1936–37

Officers

OXFORD

D. R. Wilson.	*President and Captain.*	Balliol.
G. I. Willis.	*Hon. Secretary.*	Exeter.
F. J. McLean.	*Hon. Treasurer.*	Queen's.

CAMBRIDGE

| R. R. McLernon. | *Captain.* | Trinity. |
| D. Richardson. | *Hon. Secretary.* | Trinity. |

CHAPTER VI

OLYMPIC ICE-HOCKEY, 1920, 1924, 1928, 1932 AND 1936

GREAT BRITAIN'S PART, ALSO THE HISTORY
AND IDEALS OF THE OLYMPIC GAMES

As this is an Olympic year it may be appropriate to give first of all a short sketch of the Olympic Games, with their ideals.

The Games commenced in 776 B.C. and endured for over a thousand years until A.D. 293. They were held every fourth year at Olympia and lasted in the Golden Age of Greece for seven days.

They included not only the athletic games as celebrated nowadays, but also a religious festival. The occasion was one of the greatest national gatherings of the Greeks as well as one of the rare periods of universal truce. The ancient Olympic Games have well been called " the greatest unifying force in the essentially Greek period of world's history."

All those connected with or taking part in the modern Olympic Games owe a debt of gratitude to the Baron Pierre de Courbertin, for it is to him that the reincarnation of the games is due. What greater wish can an athlete have than to represent his country where the highest honours in sport are concerned, the Olympic honours?

It has been the one wish above all others of the athletes of every nation since the inception of the Games to represent their countries in this great international festival of sport, whether in the Summer or the Winter Games. The opportunity very rarely occurs more than once or perhaps twice in the life of an amateur sportsman or woman.

The date of the first Olympiad, which centred on track and field events, was in the summer of 1896 at Athens, and, with the exception of 1916, the Olympic Games have been held every fourth year since their revival.

The only occasion on which the Games have been held in this country was in 1908.

Winter games have formed an integral part of the Olympic programme since 1924. Olympic Ice-Hockey, however, took place for the first time at Antwerp in 1920.

The Olympic ideal is World Peace, and the Games have for their object the bringing together of the various nations in friendly competition and intercourse.

The eminent President of the International Olympic Committee, Baron de Courbertin gave, as his address at the opening meeting of the committee in Rome in 1923, a very fine interpretation of the Olympic ideal. " Physical fitness, culture of what is beautiful, work for the benefit of one's family and the world in general ; that, gentlemen, is the modern Olympic goal and such is the mission that is given to the International Olympic Council to foster and propagate."

The British Olympic Association was formed in 1905, the Council of which is engaged on building up and maintaining the prestige of Britain in the world of sport. Some of the Council's endeavours are to promote by all possible means the interests of every sport and game played by the people. Further, to educate public opinion as to the importance of properly organized physical recreation in improving the health of the nation, also developing character and good citizenship.

The Britisher, in peace and war, in commerce or in sport, stands by his word and by his comrade, and it is clearly Great Britain's duty to carry on the Olympic ideal through times of difficulty and discord.

1920

Although Great Britain took no part in the Olympic matches of 1920, the history of Olympic Hockey would not be complete without reference to that year and why Great Britain was not represented.

No attempt was made to get together a British team to

go to Antwerp as there were not sufficient players available who were of a high enough standard or qualified to represent the country. Also, the matches did not take place until April 20th, by which time any qualified players who had been playing in Switzerland during the past winter would have been quite lacking in practice.

Seven countries took part in the matches. Teams from Canada and the U.S.A. visited Europe for the first time and thus great interest was naturally roused. In the first round Sweden beat Belgium 8—0. Canada beat Czechoslovakia 15—0, while the U.S.A. beat Switzerland by the colossal score of 29—0. In the second round, or semifinal, Sweden beat France, who had drawn a bye in the first round by 4—0. The other semi-final was between Canada's Winnipeg Falcons and the U.S.A. It must have been a very exciting match, for the Falcons only won 2—1 ; hundreds of people failed to obtain admission to it. The final was between Canada and Sweden. The Falcons had an easy passage and won 12—0, and so gained the first Olympic Ice-Hockey honours.

1924

The British Olympic Council being very desirous that Great Britain should be represented in the winter programme of the 1924 Games, the chairman of the Council, the late Lord Cadogan, wrote to the author on October 6th, 1923, and invited him to assist in the organization of the arrangements for the participation of our teams and individuals. He suggested the formation of a small committee consisting of experts in the various sports, and placed the offices of the British Olympic Association at the disposal of the committee. The wishes of the chairman and his Council were carried out and Great Britain was ably represented in four out of the five sports of the programmes. Ski-ing was given a miss, because in those days there were no Britishers anywhere near up to the standard of continental skiers.

Despite our having no ski-ing representatives, Great Britain did exceedingly well and gained third place out of

twelve nations that took part. The very successful display
of our Ice-Hockey team was a considerable factor in our
country's effort to gain so high a place in Olympic Winter
Games honours.

In those days the facilities for getting an Ice-Hockey
team together were nothing like what they are at present.
Manchester was the only rink in Great Britain where
hockey was played. The management of that rink kindly
placed it at the disposal of the British Ice-Hockey Association for a trial game. The Army team which had been
playing in Switzerland the previous season played The
Rest. A good game was won by The Rest 4—3. The
Army team, however, had not been on skates since the
previous winter. The following names were sent to the
British Olympic Association secretary as members of our
first Olympic Ice-Hockey team :—

> E. D. Carruthers, C. G. Carruthers, M.C., C. Ross Cuth-
> bert, M.C., H. D. Jukes, E. B. Pitblado, C. B. Boulden,
> L. H. Carr Harris, B. N. Sexton, W. H. Anderson,
> B. M. Patton, G. E. Clarkson.

The team went out to Switzerland for about a fortnight
before going to Chamonix. Several trial games took place
against Swiss teams in addition to much-needed practice ;
the result was that the play was greatly improved. G. E.
Clarkson, who played for Toronto University in 1912 and
was a member of successful British teams in Switzerland
in 1914 and 1920, acted as coach.

On the eve of the Winter Games, which began on January
25th, the thaw of the previous days, accompanied by rain,
still continued. During the night, however, a hard frost
occurred and good weather continued for the whole ten
days allotted to the Sports.

Eight countries, divided into two pools, competed for
Ice-Hockey honours.

> *Pool A.*—Canada, Czechoslovakia, Sweden and Switzer-
> land.

> *Pool B.*—Belgium, France, Great Britain, the U.S.A.

The four countries in each pool met one another and

the two leading countries from each pool composed the
final one. In this final one, however, only the countries
met who had not done so before.

The matches were played in three periods of twenty
minutes each, with ten-minute intervals. Two reserves
were allowed in those days and also a reserve goalkeeper.
As our two reserves did not produce the form anticipated
of them, the same forwards had to play throughout the
matches and were tiring in our final match, which was
against the Swedes; in consequence we only just 'got
home!'

Some huge scores were made by the North American
teams against their European opponents. Having in view
the great levelling up that has taken place since 1924 between teams from the New World and the Old, it will be of
interest to mention the enormous number of goals obtained
in the matches in which players from across the Atlantic
took part. The British team comes in this category, because all its members except two were Canadians either in
the Army or in business, and so qualified by residence over
here.

Canada	beat	Switzerland	33—0
,,	,,	Czechoslovakia	30—0
,,	,,	Sweden	22—0
U.S.A.	,,	France	22—0
,,	,,	Sweden	20—0
,,	,,	Belgium	19—0
Canada	,,	Gt. Britain	19—2
Gt. Britain	,,	Belgium	19—3
,, ,,	,,	France	15—2
U.S.A.	,,	Gt. Britain	11—0

The final match of all was between Canada (the Granites)
and the U.S.A.; it was won by the former 6—1. A splendid game, in which the two American players, 'Bobby'
Abel and Herbert Drury, the last named Canadian born,
showed up magnificently against their rivals, who were a
better-balanced team.

Drury was the best individual player as well as probably
the fastest ever seen in Europe so far. Boston daily papers

stated that ' Herb ' Drury was to Ice-Hockey what Babe
Ruth was to Baseball—' some ' testimonial !

Before the Canada *v.* U.S.A. match began the respective
goal-keepers' pads were measured by M. Paul Loicq, who
was to referee the match.

While this operation was in progress, some wit in the
crowd called out, " Why not measure the puck as well ? "

Canada had a very remarkable goal record. They obtained 110 to the 3 of their opponents. Great Britain
got two of these and was the only European team to score
more goals against their opponents than their opponents
did against them. Goals for, 40 ; goals against, 38.

Great Britain was undefeated by any European country
and therefore deserved the title of European Champions
for that year. It was hard luck that the present-day
ruling was not then in force, whereby the European country
that comes out highest in the quest for Olympic honours
gains the Championship of Europe. This Championship
was held later in the season at Milan, and it was quite
impossible to get our team together again to go there.

1928

The Second Olympic Winter Games were held at St.
Moritz from February 11th to 19th, inclusive. Holland was
the country that organized the Olympic Games this year,
but, having no facilities for the Winter ones, had delegated
them to Switzerland. Under Olympic ruling a country
unable to carry out the winter programme, after being
allotted the Olympic Games, has the power to transfer
the organization of them to a country having the necessary
facilities and being willing to hold them.

The hockey matches were noted for the splendid spirit
of give and take, the true Olympic spirit ; and the general
good feeling prevailing between all players of the various
nations was most marked. The Canadians set a high
example by playing clean, hard hockey, and one felt proud
to think that they and our team were members of the same
Empire.

The absence of an American team, through having to

scratch shortly before the games began, caused deep regret, as it did to all hockey enthusiasts in the U.S.A. To prevent a repetition occurring, the Amateur Athletic Union of the U.S., at the request of the U.S.A.H.A., which formerly exercised jurisdiction over the sport, reluctantly took over control of Ice-Hockey.

Although our team, as individuals, obtained preliminary practice at home, we lacked the necessary amount, as the Ice Club, our headquarters, was flooded in January. Added to this it was difficult to get a team together, and the two Cambridge members could only get leave for the actual days the games were in progress. Consequently, they could not join us in any preliminary practice at St. Moritz.

Eleven countries took part in the matches and were divided into two pools of three countries and one of four. Each country in a pool met the other. The final one consisted of the winner of each pool and Canada. As the Canadians were Olympic winners in 1924, it was decided to pass them straight into the final pool. Great Britain, Switzerland and Sweden won their respective pools. Our team, however, headed its pool on goal average only. We won our first match against Belgium easily but rather unexpectedly lost to France. The former country caused us a very pleasant surprise by beating France. It was left to us to decide our own fate and to beat Hungary if possible, which we just managed to do by one goal to nil. Ice conditions had been rendered none too good for the matches. Ours was the third to be played in succession, and the state of the ice surpasses description. The hot February sun after the rain of the previous day made the ice much more suitable, as our secretary, Vic Tait, very aptly described it, for use in a cocktail shaker. The 'Hockey' as played more resembled the land game than that played on ice, with a little golf thrown in. Our secretary, in giving an account of the match, said, "Skating was impossible after the first few minutes, and it developed into a hit-and-run battle with occasional tee shots by the defence!" The match had to be played to enable the programme to be finished within the time limit allowed for the completion of the Olympic Games.

In the final pool Great Britain lost to Switzerland 4—0, to the Swedes 3—1, and to Canada 14—0, so had to be content with fourth place. Although beaten by such a large margin our game with Canada, from a hockey standard point of view, was probably the best game of the series. The British team played a hard game and attacked the Canadian goal throughout, but Sullivan in goal played a wonderful game and was undefeated, as the score shows.

The British team was as follows :—

> W. G. Speechley (Cambridge) and G. Rogers (Zuoz College), goal-keepers; C. I. Wylde (Cambridge), W. Hurst Brown (London Canadians) and V. H. Tait (United Services), defence ; C. Ross Cuthbert, M.C., Captain, S. R. Carruthers, C. G. Carruthers and H. F. G. Greenwood (United Services), F. N. Melland (Manchester), B. H. Fawcett (Rosey College), forwards.

1932

Great Britain was unable to send a team to Lake Placid, where the Olympic Winter Games took place this year, for two reasons : the great expense of sending a team to the U.S.A., and had that difficulty been got over we could not have been represented by a team sufficiently strong to give a good account of itself.

Only two European countries made the journey across the Atlantic. These could not have done so but for financial support other than that accorded to teams of Great Britain which have made, or desire to make, expensive journeys abroad.

The four teams taking part in the Olympic Ice-Hockey matches played one another twice. Poland took part for the first time. The games produced much closer contests than in any previous winter Olympiad, and those between Canada and the U.S.A. were remarkably even, as the scores show :—

Canada beat U.S.A.　　2—1 and drew 2—2 ⎫
　　,,　　,,　Germany 4—1 and 5—1　　⎬ 11 Points.
　　,,　　,,　Poland　 9—0 and 10—0　　⎭

U.S.A. versus Canada, see above ⎫
   ,,   beat Germany 7—0 and 8—0 ⎬ 9 Points.
   ,,   ,,   Poland   4—1 and 5—0 ⎭

Germany versus Canada and U.S.A., see above ⎫
   ,,   beat Poland 2—1 and 4—1   ⎬ 4 Points.

Poland lost all matches, see above   0 Points.

A friend of the author who is very well informed as to Ice-Hockey form in Canada wrote to him about five weeks before the Olympic matches began, and said : " In the Olympic Games at Lake Placid I fear that we are running a chance of being beaten by the Americans. Our committee have chosen the Winnipeg team because they were champions last year, to represent Canada as a whole unit. Chances are that this year there may be six other clubs better than Winnipeg. There should be many trials of various teams and picked players from them all chosen. I think that we could still produce at least six teams in Canada equal to defeat anything from the U.S.A."

As Canada drew one match with the U.S.A. and only won the other by the odd goal in three, the writer's fears were certainly justified.

1936

On the fifth occasion of Olympic Ice-Hockey matches, which took place at Garmisch-Partenkirchen in Bavaria from February 6th to 16th, this year, Great Britain's success was a unique one.

To win the Triple Crown, Olympic Honours, the World Championship and the European Championship, is an achievement that any European country will be very hard put to to equal but can never beat. Neither American nor Canadian teams can make a similar record, because they are not eligible, of course, to hold the title of European Champions.

Thanks to the ruling that every National League team has to have a quota of English-born players, it was possible to send a team to Germany on which there were very high hopes ; some, indeed, had the highest !

A certain amount of criticism was evoked as to why our team included a number of ' Canadians.' It was thought that those players in the team who had played for some time in Canada must be Canadians.

This criticism is easily refuted ; all players who came over were English born, as proved by their birth certificates.

By Olympic ruling a player may represent the country of his birth, provided he has not become naturalized to some other country, no matter where he resides or has resided since his birth. It is, therefore, quite clear that a player born in the United Kingdom, and going to Canada when perhaps very young to reside, is of course perfectly eligible to play for his mother-country.

A blizzard prevailed at the opening ceremony just as it did eight years previously on the occasion of the Olympic Winter Games at St. Moritz. The weather, however, on the whole was quite good, though rather mild on one or two occasions, throughout the eleven days that the Games lasted. The mild days, however, could not affect the ice as at St. Moritz, thanks to artificial freezing.

The organization and carrying out of the Sports were characteristic of German thoroughness and efficiency to the last word.

Herr Hitler was present at a number of the hockey matches as well as at other competitions, together with several very highly placed government officials.

The members of our team and others were greatly pleased at getting the Führer's autograph.

On certain evenings, owing to overtime being necessary, many spectators would have had to leave before the end of the matches in order to catch the last train back to Munich. By Herr Hitler's order the trains waited until the matches were finished ; a very sporting act and much appreciated. As an English spectator remarked, " In what other country would anyone have ever thought of such a thing being done ? " Two of the matches for which the trains were delayed were those between Germany and Great Britain and Great Britain against the U.S.A.

Fifteen countries took part in the hockey matches, a

much greater number than on the last occasion the Winter Games were held in Europe, which was in 1928.

There were four eliminating pools. In Pool A. Canada beat Latvia, Poland and Austria. The last-named country, by beating Poland and Latvia, also went up into a semi-final pool with Canada.

In B. Pool the Italians, to the very great general surprise, beat the U.S.A. 2—1 ; they lost to Germany and Switzerland, however, and so did not gain promotion. Switzerland, a much fancied team, also met with two defeats, so Germany and the U.S.A. with only one defeat each went up. The latter country only beat Germany 1—0.

Hungary and Czechoslovakia gained promotion from Pool C. The first-named country scored, for these Olympic matches, the large number of eleven goals against the Belgians ; the same number as did Canada in Pool A. against Latvia.

Great Britain had only two countries to meet in Pool D. The first match, which was against Sweden, and as has nearly always been the case when the countries have met, proved a very close one, for we only won 1—0. Our other game was with Japan, and although we won 3—0, the Far-Eastern team put up a good show. As a competitor for Olympic Honours in the future the Japanese team will be still more formidable rivals. They made a close study of certain of our players in action by ocular observation and cine-camera. Their play has improved considerably since their only previous visit to Europe some six years ago, which included a visit to England.

Sweden, by beating Japan 2—0, entered a semi-final, like Great Britain.

Great Britain was drawn in semi-final Pool A. with Canada, Hungary and Germany. We first met Canada and gained the lead. Then the scores were made level, after which Brenchley got for us the goal that made history. We easily defeated Hungary 5—1 after a dull game. The match with Germany, however, was quite another matter. It was a fast, clean game. Great Britain got a goal in the second period, Germany did so in the third end, and so it was 1—1 at ' time.' Three periods of ten minutes each were then played and still no score, so points were divided. In the other two matches in this pool Canada beat Germany 6—2 and Hungary 15—0 ; this was the largest number of goals obtained by a team in any of the thirty-seven matches that took place in the Tournament. Great Britain with two wins and one draw therefore entered the final pool with Canada, who had two wins and one defeat.

In semi-final Pool B. were the U.S.A., Sweden, Czechoslovakia and Austria. The last-named country's team was again captained by Baron H. von Trauttenberg, known to many of his English friends as ' Dicky,' a defence player and very popular member of the Streatham team. His country lost to Sweden and the U.S.A. by the narrow margin of 1—0 in both matches, and were also defeated by the Czechs. The last named, as the result of their two wins over Sweden and Austria, entered the final pool together with the unbeaten U.S.A.

Canada (in whose team was J. Haggarty, a ' star ' player of the Wembley Canadians and who has made many friends since arriving in this country), the U.S.A., Great Britain and Czechoslovakia therefore constituted the final four. The Czechs and the U.S.A. having already previously met did not, according to the rules under which the tournament was played, do so again ; neither did Canada and Great Britain for the same reason.

The first final pool match was between Great Britain and Czechoslovakia on February 14th. It was one on which a great deal depended—the Championship of Europe. If we won we should at any rate secure one title and perhaps more eventually. If we lost, our hopes of any honours vanished. Should the scores have been level at the end of the allotted sixty minutes' play, overtime, of course, as in our match against Germany, would have had to be played, and up to thirty minutes if necessary. If there still had been no definite result, the winners of the Championship of Europe would not be known until Canada had met the Czechs and we and the U.S.A. had also met ; goal average would then have been the deciding factor.

Our fate was quickly settled, however, for we had a

5—0 victory over Czechoslovakia, a much easier one than had been anticipated. The game was one of the cleanest of the whole series, only one player being sent off during the match.

Next morning Canada beat the Czechs 7—0, and in the evening Great Britain and the U.S.A. met. The result of this match meant a great deal to Great Britain's chance of gaining premier honours. If we lost, we and the U.S.A. would have four points each with the remote chance of our finally winning on goal average, provided that Canada beat the U.S.A. by a certain margin.

It happened, however, that after a long-drawn-out match in which the full period of extra time was played, a goalless match was the outcome. The game was a hard one and, except on rare occasions, colourless, for both sides acted mainly on the defensive. The respective goals had narrow escapes, especially when a shot of ours hit the American goal-post, and vice versa, when only three minutes from the end of the final extra ten minutes, with Foster lying helpless on the ice, Smith shot wide. This game was also a remarkably clean one ; only one player from each side was sent off as the result of a slight scrimmage between them.

After the match it was erroneously announced at the Stadium that Great Britain had won Olympic honours. It was, however, subsequently pointed out that if the Americans could beat the Canadians without having a goal scored against them or win by more than 5—1, Olympic honours would be theirs through goal average.

On the afternoon of Sunday, February 16th, the remaining match, Canada versus the U.S.A., was played. Canada got the only goal of the game shortly after its commencement.

It was not a good match and compared poorly with the grand one between these countries on the last occasion that they met in Europe. This was in the final Olympic match at Chamonix in 1924. Several ' Old Timers ' who were present on both occasions were thoroughly agreed on this point.

The Americans missed their captain, J. Garrison, one

of their best players, who was injured in the match of the previous night. They appeared to be a tired team, and small wonder, considering that the match with Great Britain had lasted far into the night owing to full overtime having to be played. Had they not had to take part in so long-drawn-out a game so few hours previously, and also been able to have the assistance of their captain, the result might possibly have been different.

The Canadian victory enabled Great Britain to carry off Olympic honours and the World's Championship, in addition to the European previously won. It was of course the first time that these two championships had left North America. It was the second time that we had won the European Championship, the first being in 1910, the year of its inception.

Certain factors contributed very materially to our winning the Triple Crown.

The team was enabled to play several trial matches before it left England, which, it is hardly necessary to say, were of considerable benefit to it. Then to the coach, E. P. Nicklin, great credit is due ; another and very great element in our success. His tactics, especially in our match against Canada, after we had gained the lead for the second time, constituted strategy of the highest order.

Even with these two factors, success, however, could not have been attained unless all the members of our team had shown great keenness and given of their best in the desire to win. Although it is therefore perhaps invidious to single out any player for special mention, it may be permissible to refer to the grand work of Foster in goal. His many miraculous saves, especially those in our match against the U.S.A., will long be remembered by many of those who witnessed them. His work all through the various matches constituted a bulwark in our defence which most opponents found almost impregnable. In no match were more than two goals scored against him, and in the matches in which Great Britain took part the total of goals against us was only three.

To the team's captain, Carl Erhardt, great credit is also

due for the large amount of work that he has done ' behind the scenes ' as well as the part he played in his team's victories. He can retire, after nine years' association with us in the game, proudly but rightly satisfied with the great success that it has been his lot to achieve.

The placings in the final pool were :—

	Played	Won	Drawn	Lost	Goals for	Goals against	Points
Great Britain	3	2	1	0	7	1	5
Canada	3	2	0	1	9	2	4
U.S.A.	3	1	1	1	2	1	2
Czecho-slovakia	3	0	0	3	0	14	0

Explanatory note.—In the final pool each country played only two matches, for the reason stated at the beginning of the notes describing same. Each country therefore entered the final pool credited with the result of its game (including goals for and against) with the other country that it had met in the semi-final pool and which reached the final one.

It is worthy of note that in the seven matches in all that Great Britain took part in, only three goals were scored against her ; one each by Canada, Germany and Hungary. A great testimony to grand goal-keeping supported by fine defence play.

NAMES OF TEAM

J. Foster,	Goal,	Richmond Hawks.
G. Dailley,	Defence,	Wembley Lions.
C. Erhardt (Capt.),	Defence,	Streatham.
R. Wyman,	Defence,	Wembley Canadians.
J. Kilpatrick,	Left Forward,	Wembley Lions.
J. Chappell,	Centre Forward,	Earl's Court Rangers.
J. G. Davey,	Right Forward,	Streatham.
A. Archer,	Right Forward,	Wembley Lions.
J. Coward,	Left Forward,	Richmond Hawks.
E. Brenchley,	C. or R. Forward,	Streatham.
J. Borland,	Forward or Defence.	Brighton Tigers.
A. Child,	Goal,	Wembley Lions.

CHAPTER VII

HISTORY OF THE INTERNATIONAL ICE-HOCKEY LEAGUE

To Louis Magnus of Paris must be given the credit for the creation of this body. In order to do this he convened a meeting which took place in Paris on May 15th, 16th, 1908. The meeting was attended by representatives of France, Belgium, England and Switzerland ; Germany and Russia were also invited but were unable to send delegates.

The original five countries who joined in 1908 were France on October 20th, Bohemia (now Czechoslovakia) on November 15th, England on November 19th, Switzerland on November 23rd, and Belgium on December 8th.

From this modest beginning the number of countries affiliated has now reached twenty-one by the addition of the following :—Germany 1909, Oxford Canadians (as representing Canada in Europe) 1911, Sweden 1912, Canada (which country replaced the Oxford Canadians) and the United States 1920, Italy 1922, Austria, Roumania and Spain 1924, Poland 1925, Hungary 1927, Finland 1928, Japan and Latvia 1930, Newfoundland 1933, Holland and Norway 1934.

Newfoundland and Spain are, however, at the present time non-active members of the League.

The first President of the League was its founder, L. Magnus, who occupied that position until 1912, when H. Van den Bulcke (Belgium) succeeded him and carried on until 1914. Magnus was re-elected President at the Congress of Berlin in February that year but resigned at once. A special meeting of the League was held immediately afterwards and Van den Bulcke was again made President ; he, however, vacated that office in 1915. The next Congress was in 1920 at Antwerp, when M. Sillig

(Switzerland) became President. There was no meeting of the League in 1921, but in 1922 one was held at St. Moritz when Paul Loicq (Belgium) was chosen, and he has occupied the chair ever since. To have been elected to the Presidency for fifteen years in succession is a very clear token of appreciation of the extremely capable and efficient manner in which he has filled that difficult post. His profession as a barrister, consistent tact and knowledge of languages have rendered him singularly suitable for it.

The first Vice-President of the League was the author, who was elected in 1910, also in 1913, 1914 and 1923. H. Kleeberg (Germany), who has done an immense amount of work in the cause of hockey, was a Vice-President in 1911, 1932 and 1935. Except for Dr. P. Müller (Switzerland), 1925 and 1927, no one else has been a Vice-President for more than one year. H. Kleeberg organized the first International Ice-Hockey Tournament, which was in 1908 at Berlin and was won by England. Germany was not, however, a member of the International body until 1909, and so the first officially organized one by the League was that at Chamonix in 1909, which was also won by England.

Commencing with 1920 there have always been two Vice-Presidents of the League, and since 1924 one of them has always been a representative of Canada or the U.S.A.

The League Committee meets annually and normally in whichever place the Olympic or World Championship is being held. The Committee consists of one delegate from each actively affiliated country together with the President and Secretary. Three members of any country may attend the meeting but only one vote is accorded to each nation.

In André Poplimont (Belgium) the League is extremely lucky to have so universally popular a Secretary-Treasurer, and one who has rendered such valuable and efficient services in its cause for very many years ; last February he was re-elected to that office for the twelfth successive time. With the President and Secretary both of the same country and not living very far apart, as well as being such capable linguists, the working of League matters is therefore greatly facilitated.

CHAPTER VIII

STATUTES OF THE INTERNATIONAL ICE-HOCKEY LEAGUE

Art. I.—DESCRIPTION

The associations or clubs who have become signatories to the following statutes, constitute the International Ice-Hockey League (Ligue Internationale de Hockey sur Glace).

Art. II.—OBJECT

The object of the L.I.H.G. is to develop the game of Ice-Hockey, by providing a governing body and a uniform code of rules, by encouraging the formation of Associations in those countries not already having any, by making arrangements for regular international tournaments, such as the Championship of Europe and the Championship of the World and by eliminating such differences as may arise between countries affiliated to the League.

Art. III.—MEMBERS (Active and Honorary)

Every country wherein Ice-Hockey is played can become affiliated as an ' active member ' of the L.I.H.G. under the reservations and conditions stated below.

Every country where Ice-Hockey is not played can become affiliated as an ' honorary member ' under the same reservations and conditions.

Any active member who ceases to take an active part in Ice-Hockey may apply to become an honorary member only.

Active members will be admitted in a consultative and executive capacity, honorary members in a consultative capacity only.

Art. IV.—AFFILIATION

1. No country can become affiliated to the L.I.H.G. save through the association which governs its games in general or its Ice-Hockey in particular. Where no such association exists all the clubs can become directly affiliated themselves, but their affiliation becomes void on the formation of an association acknowledged by the L.I.H.G.

2. Requests for affiliation imply a formal undertaking to abide by the statutes and rules of the L.I.H.G., and should be addressed to the President of the L.I.H.G. together with two copies, either in French or English, of the statutes and rules of the association or the club seeking affiliation.

If the nation possessing the association or the club sponsors the request for affiliation, the said association or club never having been previously refused affiliation and having, in the opinion of the President, nothing in its statutes or rules contrary to those of the L.I.H.G., then affiliation with all the rights and duties pertaining thereto may be granted provisionally by the President, who shall give notice of such affiliation both to the club or association and to the members of the committee of the L.I.H.G.

During the month following the receipt of the circular from the President giving notice of the provisional affiliation, the members of the committee shall send in their report to the President, stating their reasons in case of non-acquiescence.

If the majority report favourably, or if no report is received within the said month, the acquiescence of the members can be taken for granted and affiliation will become absolute; if otherwise, the President will suspend affiliation by giving notice to the club or association of the grounds on which the objection is based and will bring forward the question at the next meeting of the congress, at which a delegate from the said club or association will be invited to attend and present his case in order that the question may then be definitely settled by a majority vote.

3. The associations or clubs affiliated to the L.I.H.G. shall be recognised as the sole governing authorities of the game of Ice-Hockey within their respective countries.

4. On a vote of seventy-five per cent. of the committee any nation, association or club can be excluded from affiliation with the L.I.H.G. Notice of appeal may be laid before the congress.

Art. V.—HEADQUARTERS

The Headquarters of the L.I.H.G. shall be the residence of the President in office.

Art. VI.—SOCIAL YEAR

The League functions from the conclusion of one congress until the conclusion of the congress following.

Art. VII.—SUBSCRIPTIONS

1. The yearly subscription is fixed for active members at 100 *Swiss francs gold* for each country and for honorary members at 10 *Swiss francs gold*.

2. In the case where there is a national association, this association will be responsible for the subscription. Where there is no national association, clubs will each pay a subscription proportionate to their number.

3. *Subscriptions shall be paid in advance, not later than the commencement of the annual congress, at the roll-call. Any association in default at that time shall forfeit its right of vote at the congress. The latter shall consider whether such association should be excluded from championship games. Such association shall, moreover, be liable,* after due notice has been given, to expulsion from the League. Finally, subscriptions which are not paid by the end of the

congress shall carry interest at the rate of one per cent. per month ; each fraction of a month counting as one month.

Art. VIII.—JURISDICTION

The L.I.H.G. is governed by :
(1) The Executive Committee ;
(2) The General Committee ;
(3) The International Congress.

Art. IX.—COMMITTEES

1. The general committee is constituted each year from the delegates sent by the affiliated countries, each country sending one delegate.

2. The congress elects by secret ballot, and not in the presence of the delegates, a President, a first Vice-President from Europe and a second Vice-President from America, who shall act with full power, the one for the other, in order of priority, and who, together with the Secretary-Treasurer, constitute the executive committee.

3. The President shall elect the Secretary-Treasurer on his own responsibility.

4. If the office of President falls vacant during the term, the first Vice-President, or failing him the second Vice-President, will exercise his functions until the next congress.

5. If a member of the general committee sends in his resignation, he will be replaced by another delegate elected by the association to which the member belonged.

6. Each country becoming affiliated during the interval between two congresses shall have the right to send a delegate to the general committee.

7. Members of the general committee shall no longer function as such on ceasing to be members of an association or club affiliated to the L.I.H.G.

ART. X.—COMPETENCE (President and Committee)

1. Such matters as are not especially reserved to the congress shall be left to the discretion of the executive committee, particularly : the carrying out of the decisions of the congress ; ratification of the choice of referees for international matches proposed by the affiliated associations or clubs ; co-ordination of the results of tournaments and championships ; control of finance ; preparations for and convocation of the congress ; the admission or exclusion of a nation, association, or club ; adjudication in disputes between affiliated countries ; appeals in regard to the statutes and regulations ; the interpretation of the rules of Ice-Hockey, etc.

2. The executive committee shall base its decisions on the results of circulars, addressed by the executive committee to the members of the general committee, and returned to it, active members giving their vote for or against, honorary members giving their comments on the subject-matter. If a delegate has not replied within one month from the date of the receipt of the circular he will be considered to have ratified the majority vote.

3. Nevertheless, the President may act alone and on his own responsibility in the following cases :—

(a) Disagreement between affiliated countries as to the date for the organization of international tournaments ;

(b) Financial arrangements ;

(c) Co-ordination of results and contests ;

(d) Preparation for and calling of the congress ;

(e) Provisional affiliation ;

(f) Appeals *re* statutes and regulations ;

(g) Interpretation of the rules of Ice-Hockey ;

(h) In general all questions of ordinary routine in addition to all those questions requiring urgent decisions, provided his decision in respect of (g) above is duly ratified by the general committee.

4. Affiliated clubs and associations may lodge an appeal with the congress from all decisions given by the President or the executive committee.

5. The League is only bound by engagements signed or endorsed by the President.

6. The decisions of the President and the committee, as well as all notices and circulars, will be published in the official booklet of the L.I.H.G. Each affiliated country may have its own official organ in which it may insert the official communications of the L.I.H.G. on the responsibility of the delegates of each nation.

Art. XI.—MEETINGS

1. The ordinary international meeting of the congress will be held each year on the occasion of the Championship of Europe or of the World and will be called by the President on at least one month's notice before the actual date of the meeting.

2. An extraordinary meeting of the congress can be called at any time at the request of the majority of the affiliated countries. Similar methods of procedure to those adopted for the ordinary meetings of congress obtain in the case of an extraordinary meeting.

3. Only the delegates of affiliated associations or clubs may take part in the congress. No delegate may represent more than two countries at a time.

4. Each country may send three delegates, but shall only be entitled to one vote, whether represented by one association or by a number of clubs. In the latter case, the clubs shall decide among themselves on the choice of their delegates. Countries who are only honorary members may act only in a consultative capacity at the congress.

No association being in arrears with its subscription, as laid down in Art. VI above, shall have the right to vote at the congress ; this clause shall be strictly applied.

5. Resolutions are passed by the vote of the majority present. The President has the casting vote in the case of a tie.

6. Among the duties of the congress may be noted the following :—

(a) To approve the report of the President and that of the Secretary-Treasurer and to approve the profit and loss account ;

(b) To discuss and vote on proposed modifications of the statutes or regulations or in the rules of play provided such modifications appear on the Agenda drawn up by the President, to whom they shall have been addressed at least two months before the date of the congress ;

(c) To decide questions of opposition to the absolute affiliation of an association or club, as laid down in Section 2 of Art. IV ;

(d) To delegate the arrangements for the Championships of Europe and of the World to one of the associations or clubs who have made application, designating at the same time three nations at least who shall be chosen in default of one another and in the order of priority determined by congress ;

(e) To ratify the exclusion of an affiliated association or club in case of such an application from them ;

(f) To discuss and vote on various questions which are not included in sub-section (6) of this section ;

(g) To elect the President and the vice-Presidents.

7. All persons who shall have been properly elected as delegates to represent their association at a congress may obtain an official L.I.H.G. badge. These badges, which shall be numbered and for which the holders shall be responsible, shall entitle them to free access to any match, tournament or championship organized under the rules of the L.I.H.G. by an affiliated association or club belonging to such association.

Authority to wear this badge shall be certified by a

special identity card, signed by the Secretary of the L.I.H.G., and bearing a photograph of the holder, certified by his national federation.

Art. XII.—DISSOLUTION

The dissolution of the L.I.H.G. shall only be effected by the majority vote at a meeting of the congress called especially for the purpose.

The general committee will then appoint a liquidator and will dispose of the funds.

Royal Family watching ice hockey match at Hengler's rink, 4th Feb 1904.
Left to right: Queen Sophie of Norway, King Oscar II of Norway, Princess
Victoria, Prince of Wales (later George V), Queen Alexandra, King Edward VII,
Princess Of Wales (later Queen Mary), Duke of Connaught.

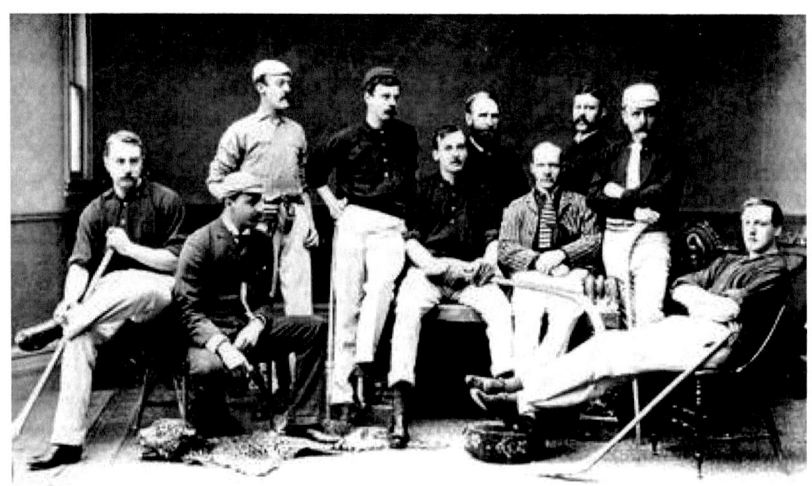

"The Rebels"

C1

England (all white) v Belgium in European Championship at Les Avants,
Switzerland in 1910

JJ Cawthra (left) founder of the Inter Varsity match and P Loicq, President of
the LIHG in an international tournament at St Moritz in 1913

Streatham (National League winners 1934-35) v The Rest, October 1935

Anglo-Scottish teams, March 1936

The Great Britain Olympic team that won the gold medal at the 1936 Winter Olympics. Back row (l to r): Percy Nicklin (Coach), Bob Wyman, Archie Stinchcombe, Carl Erhardt (C), Jack Kilpatrick, Gordon Dailley, Gerry Davey, Jimmy Chappell, Edgar Brenchley, Johnny Coward. Front row (l to r): Jimmy Borland, Art Child, Jimmy Foster, Alex "Sandy" Archer. (Photo by Planet News)

The Wembley Lions
Winners of the National League and London-Paris club tournament, 1936

CHAPTER IX

BYE-LAWS OF THE L.I.H.G.

International Ice-Hockey League (Ligue Internationale de Hockey sur Glace)

Art. I.—APPLICATION

1. The present regulations are peculiar to Ice-Hockey, which is played with a puck, and not bandy, which is played with a ball.

The L.I.H.G. shall control only male hockey players.

2. No international match may be played save under the regulations of the L.I.H.G. Any club playing under different regulations may be excluded from the L.I.H.G., except by agreement between the two teams on a modification of detail, such as the duration of the game, the extra time to be played, or the number of players.

Art. II.—DEFINITION OF AN AMATEUR

Affiliated associations or clubs shall be composed of amateurs only, namely, players of hockey or team managers ; professionals can only be coaches, trainers, or medical attendants, but can never serve on the committee of the L.I.H.G.

A. A hockey player shall be regarded as a professional, who

   (a) has played or taught Ice-Hockey in consideration of direct or indirect pecuniary gain ;

   (b) is regarded as a professional or has been disqualified as an amateur by any national or international sports association whatever, for any reason whatever ;

(c) has sold or pledged any prize awarded to him in respect of sporting events ;

(d) has knowingly played against professionals in matches or official tournaments except in official training matches intended for the practice of players.

B. Amateurs may receive only

(a) prizes, cups, medals, etc., but never prizes in money ;

(b) reimbursement for travelling expenses ;

(c) reimbursement for hotel expenses during a tournament, and this for a maximum of eight days' training before the tournament ;

(d) his equipment necessary for the game, which will always remain the property of his club ;

(e) his pay while on leave, if such leave was granted under the usual circumstances or normally for the purpose of participation in the Olympic Games or European or World Championships, and provided that this be not an indirect method of securing a direct refund of pay lost. Reimbursement is strictly limited and can only be made through an association or club.

C. Professionals may regain amateur status on a request from their national Ice - Hockey association, on condition :

(a) they have been reinstated by the international association of the sports in which they had been professionals ;

(b) they have not acted as professionals in Ice-Hockey for over five years.

ART. III.—CLAIMS

1. Notice of appeal against the qualification of a player or of a team should be addressed in writing to the President of the L.I.H.G., either before the tournament or match

or within fifteen days of its completion. The complaint will be submitted by the President to the members of the general committee.

2. Any interested person is competent to lay a complaint in respect of Section 1 of this Article.

3. Without prejudice to the President's right of enforcing the statutes and regulations of the L.I.H.G., even by precautionary measures, the general committee may, if the complaint be proved, take what action it may consider necessary not only against the association or club actually at fault but also against such associations or clubs as have knowingly agreed to take part in a tournament or match organized by the association or club at fault.

Art. IV.—NATIONAL MATCHES, TOURNAMENTS AND CHAMPIONSHIPS

1. National championships, meetings, tournaments and matches organized between clubs of a particular country do not come under the jurisdiction of the L.I.H.G. Nevertheless, affiliated nations may solicit the patronage of the L.I.H.G. for the organization of the said championships, tournaments, meetings and matches on the condition that in that case they adhere to the statutes and regulations.

2. The members of the L.I.H.G. shall send to the President at the end of the Ice-Hockey season results as complete as possible of their national championships.

Art. V.—INTERNATIONAL MATCHES AND TOURNAMENTS

1. All international tournaments fixtures, and matches, and in particular the Championships of Europe and of the World, come under the jurisdiction of the L.I.H.G.

2. Only the L.I.H.G. committee or clubs affiliated with national associations belonging to the League, the said associations and delegates being specially appointed by the latter, but no commercial organizations, may arrange

international matches and organize international tournaments.

3. No affiliated association or club may take part in an international tournament, fixture or match with a non-affiliated association or club. Nevertheless, a club belonging to a nation affiliated may, with the sole view of helping its training, engage with a club belonging to a neighbouring non-affiliated nation in a friendly match, and on the express condition that the match does not rank as an international meeting or as a match played under the regulations of the L.I.H.G. This exception cannot be extended under any circumstances to a tournament.

4. In tournaments, competitions and international matches, other than World, European and Olympic Championships, the questions of nationality laid down in Section 4, Art. VI below, shall not have effect. However:

(a) No player may change his association (that is to say, play under the colours of a different association or of a club belonging to a different association) without the authorization in writing of the association to which he formerly belonged. The player shall be required to produce this authorization to his new association and the latter shall be bound to insist upon its production. Any player or association not complying with this rule shall be liable to penalty. Should the original association refuse to give this authorization, a player who considers himself wronged shall have the right to appeal to the L.I.H.G., which body shall have final decision, taking into consideration that only a real and permanent change of residence and not a change for reason of sport shall be given as reason by the player ; moreover, any player who has been penalized (suspended) by an association shall remain under such penalty with the association under whose colours he shall play henceforward. If struck off, he shall no longer play for any association.

(b) Every team described as ' National ' (*i.e.* Belgium, Belgian National, Belgian selection, etc.) shall be composed solely of players qualified to play for this national team in the L.I.H.G. Championships (laid down in Art. VI, Section 4 below). Any team containing even one player ineligible to play in the L.I.H.G. Championships under the national colours of that team, shall include in its title the word ' International ' (*e.g.* International Belgian Team, International Belgian selection, etc.) ;

(c) No team may take part in any tournament, match, or international meeting if it contains more than two ' strangers,' that is, two players who would not be authorized to play in the national team of the federation to which this team belongs. An exception may be made to this rule, provided all the interested parties are in agreement.

5. The members of the L.I.H.G. shall send to the President, before the first of October each year, the dates and conditions under which they propose to hold the international tournaments they have organized. The international programme for the season will then be sent to all members during the first fortnight of October. Members so desiring shall arrange mutually for alterations on account of fixtures clashing, and shall notify the President, who will communicate to members the alterations in the fixture list thus affected.

6. Every association or club withdrawing within eight days of the date of a match or within fifteen days of the date of a tournament, after having formally agreed to take part in the said match or tournament, is liable to a fine which shall be agreed on between the clubs at the time match or tournament is arranged.

7. In case of disagreement, the general committee of the L.I.H.G. shall be sole judge of the applicability of the fine, and the contending parties shall forward on to the committee all relevant correspondence which has passed

between the clubs. The fine shall be paid to the executive committee of the L.I.H.G., who will pass it to the beneficiary club. Where the club penalized refuses to pay the fine imposed, the general committee of the L.I.H.G. can disqualify it until it shall have paid the fine and forbid the other members of the L.I.H.G. to meet that club in any match whatsoever.

8. Similarly, should a club organizing a match or tournament, after formally accepting fixtures from one or more teams, come to cancel or postpone the match or tournament for any reason, then that club shall be liable to a fine, which shall be fixed in advance, for the benefit of the teams taking part, provided that cancellation involves pecuniary losses to the clubs engaged. The procedure and penalties shall be as laid down in Section 7 above.

9. The general committee shall at all times take into account unforeseen circumstances.

10. Members of the L.I.H.G. shall forward to the President results, as full as possible, of all the international matches or tournaments organized by them, within the month following these events. The L.I.H.G. shall each year, after the end of the season, send a résumé of the results of the national and international events to all members.

Art. VI.—EUROPEAN AND WORLD CHAMPIONSHIPS

1. The Championships of Europe and of the World can only be organized by the countries granted that privilege by the congress, which shall satisfy itself that these countries have at their disposal an artificial ice skating rink, the dimensions of which permit of the organization of these championships.

The World Championship may only be determined when a representative team from a non-European country takes part.

2. The Championships of Europe and of the World shall as far as possible be determined each year ; nevertheless, during the years when the Championship of the World is determined in Europe, the Championship of Europe shall not be played also, but the champion country of Europe shall be that European country which obtains the highest place in the Championship of the World. Furthermore, in the case of the Olympic Games the Olympic Championship shall decide the World and European Championships.

No other international match shall be played on days when these championships take place nor during the fortnight immediately preceding, except with the express consent of the President of the L.I.H.G., to whom a request shall be made in reasonable time and who shall decide if the match or tournament requested is likely to interfere with the proper organization of the said championships.

These championships may take place on enclosed or open rinks.

Instructions relative to the organization of these championships shall be communicated by the country organizing them to all the clubs or associations who are directly affiliated to the L.I.H.G. No country may enter for these championships save through the representative of its national association sitting on the general committee of the L.I.H.G.

The organizing country shall, before the first of July, notify the President and members of the League of the date chosen by it for the Championship of Europe or of the World. This date must always be after January 15th.

Sections 6 and 7 of Art. V (above) will not apply, but in the specific case of the Championships of Europe and of the World, countries who enter for the said championships will be required, under penalty of invalidating their entry, to send therewith a cheque for 100 Swiss francs gold, payable to the order of the L.I.H.G. In the event of their taking part in the championship, or cancelling their entry prior to the closing date, the cheque will be returned by the organizers. But should cancellation of their entry take place after entries close, the 100 Swiss francs gold will be retained by the L.I.H.G. by way of penalty.

The organizing country shall be required to invite at least fourteen players and two officials per team, that is, sixteen persons in all, for the European and World Championships. When the European and World Championships are included in the Olympic Championships, the Olympic rules shall apply.

The congress may forbid any country which has failed to pay its subscription to take part in championship games, without such country having any right to claim damages. (Art. VII, Section 3 of Statutes.)

3. These championships can be carried out either by pool or by elimination or by a combination of the two systems, at the discretion of the organizing country, but with the following restrictions :

(a) if there are only six teams or less taking part, the championships must, except for unforeseen circumstances, be carried out in one pool ;

(b) where the system of elimination only or the combination of systems is chosen, the organizers must take as the heads of series, for the World Championship the teams that have gained the first two places in the previous World Championship and those that have gained the first two places in the previous European Championship ; for the Championship of Europe those teams that have obtained the first four places in the previous European Championship ;

(c) in the combined system, elimination being made by pools, each group must comprise a minimum of three teams ;

(d) whichever system is adopted, the same team cannot be called on to play two matches in one day except with the consent of the captain.

The composition of the groups, whether by pool or by elimination, shall (after making provision for the heads of series) be decided by a draw, which shall take place the day before the championship at a place and hour which shall be notified at least a fortnight before to the countries participating, who may arrange to have a delegate to represent them there. The order of the matches is left to the entire discretion of the organizing committee, who shall not, however, knowingly give any advantage to their own team.

4. The following shall have the right to represent a country in the Championships of Europe and the World :—

(a) Those who possess the nationality of the said country, by birth or by naturalization ;

(b) those who do not possess this nationality but who during preceding championships have been authorized to represent the said country under rules now repealed ;

(c) those born in the Dominions, who may represent the sovereign State, and those born in the sovereign State, who may represent the Dominions ; but only on condition of residence in the sovereign State or Dominion respectively during the five consecutive years immediately preceding the competition in which they intend to take part.

When once a player has represented any nation whatsoever (sovereign State or Dominion) in the Championships of Europe or of the World he will not be allowed to represent another nation in subsequent Championships of Europe or of the World.

The birth-qualification and the five years' residence clause shall be attested by the authorities controlling sport and by the administration of the nation interested, through the medium of a committee composed of one member of the executive committee, one member of the organizing committee and one delegate from each team entered ; this committee will only have power of investigation and any objections must be laid before the congress ; verification shall take place immediately before the draw provided for in the final paragraph of Art. VI, Section 3.

5. The L.I.H.G. present silver challenge cups of the

value of five hundred gold francs for the Championships
of Europe and of the World. Each of these cups will be
presented to the official delegate of the winning nation,
who shall have charge of it until the next championship
meeting. Each cup becomes the absolute property of a
nation when such nation shall have won the championship
to which the cup belongs three times, whether consecutively
or not.

In addition the League will present to the champion
team fourteen silver-gilt medals and to the second team
fourteen silver medals, for the Championship of the World
as well as for that of Europe.

6. The games for the Championships of Europe or of the
World shall be refereed by international neutral referees,
chosen by the association or club organizing the tournament.

Appeals against the choice of referees shall be settled by
the general committee of the L.I.H.G. These appeals shall
not interfere with, stop, or hold back the order of the
games, nor alter the results obtained, but the general
committee of the L.I.H.G. may in serious cases suspend
absolutely or temporarily the association or club organizing
the tournament, and the indicted referee, or one of them
only.

7. In the Championships of Europe and of the World,
and, except where the organizing committee decides
otherwise, in international tournaments, points will be
allotted as follows :—

Match won . . .	2 points
Match drawn . . .	1 point
Match lost . . .	Nil

Any team which does not appear on the rink with at
least four players after a maximum period of a quarter
of an hour from the time fixed for the match, will be
scratched and the opposing side will be awarded the two
points for a win ; it will also be considered as having won
by 5 goals to 0 ; this rule, both in regards the number of
players and the delay of a quarter of an hour, shall only be

applied if the opposing team makes formal demand to the umpire.

Placing is done by the addition of the points, the highest number of points denoting the winner.

In case of equality between two or more teams, a replay between them will take place. If it is impossible for this replay to take place, the positions will be settled by the goal average system : the total number of goals scored in this section of the tournament by each team will be divided by the total number of goals scored against it, and the positions will be settled in accordance with the quotients thus obtained. In the event of the quotients giving to two or more teams infinity, nil or equality, such teams would be placed in proportion to the results obtained by subtracting the goals scored against from the goals scored for. If this results in a further tie, the team scoring the highest number of goals shall be given preference over the team or teams who scored less. If the teams have scored the same number of goals and it is impossible to differentiate between them merely on the basis of their scores against each other, one replay shall take place, irrespective of any difficulties in the way. In calculating the goal average, only those goals shall count which were scored in the three periods of play, those scored during extra time being omitted from the total.

8. The association or club organizing the Championships of Europe or of the World shall send to the President, during the month following the championship, the full results together with reports on the games and the referees' reports (framed as shown in Appendix 5).

ART. VII.—ACCESS TO MATCHES

Free admission shall be granted to holders of the badge described in Section 7, Art. XI of the Statutes, by the organizers of matches, tournaments and national or international Ice-Hockey championships played under the regulations of the L.I.H.G. Authority to wear this badge shall be certified by a special identity card signed by the

Secretary of the L.I.H.G., and bearing a photograph of the holder, certified by his National Federation.

ART. VIII.—EXTENSION OF PENALTIES

1. Any player who has been suspended within one federation shall bear this penalty in every affiliated federation in which he may henceforth be included, if the extension of the suspension is required from the L.I.H.G. by the federation which has imposed it.

2. If struck off he will no longer be able to play for any federation or group forming part of an affiliated federation.

3. The federation which asks for the extension of a suspension or ban shall forward to the President of the L.I.H.G. with the request :—

(*a*) The full name of the player.

(*b*) The name of the combination of which he was a member when penalized.

(*c*) The duration of the suspension.

(*d*) The date on which the player was notified thereof and from which in consequence the suspension commences.

(*e*) The reasons for suspension or striking off.

4. The L.I.H.G. will circulate the above information (with the exception of sub-section (*d*), reason for suspension) to all the affiliated federations.

5. The player so penalized shall have the right of appeal to the President of the L.I.H.G., who shall make his decision without delay and communicate it both to the player concerned and to all the affiliated federations.

6. An appeal lodged by the player does not connote suspension of the penalty, which will continue in force.

CHAPTER X

RULES OF ICE-HOCKEY

NOTE

ART. 1.—This code of rules is only a synthesis of the previous rules, together with certain alterations made by the congresses of the L.I.H.G., the whole being completed by the addition of established practice, and arranged in a more rational order than previously.

ART. 2.—Ice-Hockey originated in Canada and should not be confounded with 'Bandy.' It is played on an ice rink between two teams of six members each who wear ice skates and push or slide by means of a Stick the Puck, which they try to get through the Goal of the opponents. The Match is played during a specified Time and the team which has scored most goals is the winner. A Referee (or two) is entrusted with the enforcement of the rules, watches over the game, and is helped by Timekeepers and Goal Umpires.

1. EQUIPMENT

A. THE RINK

ART. 3.—The dimensions of the rink shall be at least 18 metres (60 feet) by 50 metres (165 feet), and at the most 33½ metres (110 feet) by 76 metres (250 feet). These proportions shall in every case be adhered to. The ideal dimensions of a rink shall be 26 metres (85 feet) by 56 metres (185 feet).

ART. 4.—The goals shall be placed at each end of the rink in the middle of the small side, the open part facing the centre, the goal line being parallel to the base line and at a distance of 1.50 m. (5 feet) minimum, and 4.50 m.

(15 feet) maximum from it (according to the length of the rink).

ART. 5.—(*a*) A line of dark colour, 2.5 cm. (1 inch) wide shall be traced on or in the ice between the posts of each goal.

(*b*) Parallel to the goal-line, lines at least 5 cm. (2 inches) wide shall be traced across the whole width of the ice in the following places :

When the rink is 60 metres (200 feet) or more long, at 18 metres (60 feet) from the goal line ;

When the rink is less than 60 metres (200 feet) long, at one-third of the distance separating the two goal-lines.

These lines, known as ' blue lines ' or ' zone lines,' shall divide the rink into three zones, known respectively as ' defence zone,' ' neutral or centre zone ' and ' attacking zone,' the latter being for each team the zone containing the opposing goal.

(*c*) A dark circle 30 cm. (1 foot) in diameter shall be marked out in the centre of the rink, that is to say, at the intersection of the imaginary diagonals.

(*d*) A circle of 3 m. (10 feet) radius, having as centre the middle of the goal-line and consisting of a stripe 5 cm. (2 inches) in width, shall be drawn around the goal, terminated behind it by a line running parallel to the goal-line and at a distance of 0.55 m. (22 inches) therefrom. (See Appendix 6.)

(The facing point for the special penalty imposed by Art. 119 shall be on the outer rim of this circle, perpendicular to the goal-line at its centre point.)

(*e*) A dark line shall be painted on the side boards defining the beginning of the end boards 5 metres (15 feet) from each goal-post (limit point for defence players to approach the face-off in case of application of the penalty specified in Art. 119).

ART. 6.—The rink shall be surrounded by a boarding which will form its limits. These boards shall be 25 cm.

(10 inches) minimum in height and the corners of the rink shall as far as possible be rounded.

B. THE GOALS

ART. 7.—The goals shall consist of two vertical posts, 122 cm. (4 feet) in height and 183 cm. (6 feet) apart, the tops of which shall be connected by a horizontal bar.

ART. 8.—A cage, the front of which is formed by this framework, will support nets sufficiently strong to resist a powerful shot. This cage will be 40 cm. (16 inches) deep at the top, and at the bottom along the ice 55 cm. (22 inches).

The upper part of the goal shall be covered by netting, like the back and sides, and by nothing else that might obstruct the view of the goal umpire.

ART. 9.—The posts shall be fixed firmly in the ice and a dark line traced between them.

ART. 10.—In the event of the goal-net being torn or the posts broken or displaced, the umpire shall stop the game, which will be resumed only when the necessary repairs have been effected.

ART. 11.—It shall be the duty of the umpire to measure the goals on the occasion of each match.

ART. 12.—The home team shall be responsible for the marking of the rink and fixing of goals. The referee shall not allow the game to commence until these rules have been strictly carried out.

C. THE PUCK

ART. 13.—The puck is a flat round disc made of hardened vulcanized rubber measuring 2.54 cm. (1 inch) in thickness by 7.62 cm. (3 inches) in diameter. Its weight shall not be less than 141.5 grammes (5 ounces) nor more than 170 grammes (6 ounces).

D. THE STICKS

ART. 14.—The sticks are square in section, and terminated at the lower end by a flat blade making an obtuse angle with the handle. They must not exceed 9 cm. (3¼ inches) in width at any part. The length of the flat blade must not exceed 38 cm. (15 inches). The total length of the handle must not exceed 137 cm. (54 inches). These sticks are made entirely of wood, tape binding being permissible.

E. THE GOAL-KEEPING PADS

ART. 15.—The goal-keeper's pads are worn essentially for protection and are not intended to give him undue assistance in keeping goal.

The pad is placed round the leg and must not constitute a shield projecting on each or one side of the leg.

ART. 16.—When the two legs are together the pads must not under any circumstances take up more than 50 cm. (20 inches) in width.

ART. 17.—The umpire shall measure the pads before the match. He is entitled to do so at any time during the match.

F. THE PLAYERS' EQUIPMENT

ART. 18.—The players, including the goal-keeper, may be provided with equipment for protection, but in no case with equipment that might give them any assistance during the match, or be capable of wounding another player. The other players shall not use the goal-keeper's equipment (with the exception of his stick as laid down in Art. 25).

G. THE OFFICIAL ENCLOSURES

ART. 19.—An official enclosure shall be reserved for the officials and timekeepers close to the rink in the centre of the longer side. All necessary facilities shall be provided in it for the timekeepers, who shall be so placed as never to lose sight of the referee at any time during the game.

ART. 20.—Another enclosure shall be reserved at the rinkside for the substitutes and penalty timekeeper. Other than these the team managers only are allowed access to this enclosure.

ART. 21.—Behind each goal enclosures shall be reserved for the goal umpire, who shall remain alone.

II. THE PLAYERS

A. THEIR POSITIONS

ART. 22.—A team is formed of six players, named according to the position they occupy in the game : three forwards (right wing, left wing and centre), two defence (left and right) and one goal-keeper.

B. SUBSTITUTES

ART. 23.—In addition to the above-mentioned six players each team may have four additional players as substitutes, who will replace the players when desired but only under the circumstances mentioned below. At no time, however, may there be more than six players per team on the rink.

ART. 24.—Furthermore, it is also permissible to have a reserve goal-keeper, but the latter may only play in goal and the substitution may only be made at the beginning of a new period, or should occasion arise during the game if the goal-keeper has been the victim of an accident which in the opinion of the referee is sufficiently severe to prevent him from continuing to play ; as soon as he has recovered, the referee shall authorize him to resume his place.

Any team whose goal-keeper has been injured shall return to the rink within not more than fifteen minutes after the interruption of the game (with the same or another goal-keeper) on penalty of forfeiting the match.

ART. 25.—Should the goal-keeper be penalized he shall be replaced by one of the players on the rink during the whole time of his enforced absence. The said player shall be authorized to play in the position of the goal-keeper, but shall not use any of the goal-keeper's equipment except his stick.

C. Substitutions

Art. 26.—A substitution may only be made during a stoppage of play, no matter what may be the reason for making the substitution.

Art. 27.—The referee must be advised of the impending substitution.

Art. 28.—In case of violation of these rules, the referee will impose the following penalties: two minutes' penalty for the two players who have carried out a substitution while the play was proceeding, or two minutes for the captain of the team having more than six players on the rink.

Art. 29.—The substitutes must be ready to play and must take their place in the team without delaying the game.

Art. 30.—The replaced player shall leave the rink simultaneously with the entry of the substitute.

Art. 31.—When not playing, the substitutes must cover their sweaters, so that the referee shall not mistake them for the players on the rink.

Art. 32.—If, from one of the two sides, more than four players (the goal-keeper excepted) are obliged to retire due to accidents, and if, consequently, it will no longer be possible to have six players on the rink, the other team will take off one or more players in order to equalize the strength of the sides on the rink.

D. Reserves

Art. 33.—The organizers of the meeting will fix the total number of players which will be admitted to take part in the meeting, on the understanding that, in accordance with Art. 23, only eleven players, inclusive of the four substitutes and the substitute goal-keeper, may be appointed for the one match. In cases where the organizers have not fixed this number, the teams may have a reserve for each player.

For World, European and Olympic Championships, the number of reserve players shall not exceed three.

E. NUMBERING

ART. 34.—All the players will be numbered and will carry the number prominently on their backs.

F. COLOURS

ART. 35.—While in play the teams will be attired in distinctly different colours, so as to avoid all confusion.

ART. 36.—Only the goal-keepers are exempt from wearing these colours which must be uniformly worn by all other members of the team.

ART. 37.—If two teams are found by the referee to be wearing colours which in his opinion are likely to prove confusing in play, the home club or alternatively the club drawn by lot will change colours.

G. THE CAPTAIN OF THE TEAM

ART. 38.—Each team shall appoint a captain from among its members.

ART. 39.—He will wear on the right arm, between the elbow and the shoulder, an armlet of a different colour from the rest of his attire bearing the letter ' C.'

ART. 40.—The captain commands the other players : he is their official representative and takes all necessary decisions in the name of the team.

ART. 41.—He tosses up for the choice of ends, and if successful makes the choice.

Art. 42.—He decides in conjunction with the referee and the opposing captain upon the deviations from the rules necessitated by unforeseen circumstances, interpretations, prolongations, cancellations, the duration of periods, etc. ; but in the case of non-agreement the ruling of the referee shall be final.

Art. 43.—After the match, he will submit any complaints which he considers well founded.

Art. 44.—If the occasion arises he ' scratches.'

III. THE OFFICIALS

A. Referee

Art. 45.—The referee is in absolute control of the game.

Art. 46.—He settles indisputably all matters in accordance with the rules of the game. He judges all disputes and makes the necessary decisions. In cases where no rules are applicable, he will act in accordance with usual practice and his own judgment.

Art. 47.—There is no appeal against the decisions of the referee. Any complaint against him, properly submitted, can have no consequence other than punishment (suspension or disqualification) if he is found to have acted wrongfully ; it can never lead to a cancellation of his decisions.

Art. 48.—The referee is appointed by the organizers.

Art. 49.—His appointment cannot be contested if he is recognized as an international referee by the L.I.H.G.

Art. 50.—He must be neutral: if, however, it is impossible to obtain a neutral referee, then the appointment is subject to agreement between the captains of the teams.

Art. 51.—The referee appoints the timekeepers and the goal umpires, selecting them so far as is feasible from neutrals. He is responsible for them and may change them at any stage of the game. He is in no wise bound to follow their advice, and will settle out of hand any dispute regarding their duties.

ART. 52.—He will come to agreement with the captains of the teams regarding the interpretation of the rules and any alterations to be made in them owing to circumstances.

ART. 53.—He will referee with the necessary severity to ensure a correct game, free from rough play or deliberate infringements.

ART. 54.—He will move with the play.

ART. 55.—His duties are principally as follows :—

(a) *Before the Match :*

1. He will confirm that the lines of the rink are properly drawn on the ice and, if necessary, will have them altered and re-drawn.

2. He will examine the equipment of the players, the pucks (of which there shall be at least two), the pads of the goal-keeper, the sticks, the goals, the numbering and the identity of the players.

3. He will examine the enclosures reserved for the officials, the substitutes, and the goal umpires, and will ensure that none but authorized persons have access to same.

4. He will appoint the other officials, see that they are provided with the necessary instruments and that they are in their places, *i.e.* two ordinary and one or more penalty timekeepers, equipped with timepieces and ready in the enclosure reserved for them ; two goal umpires, one at each end behind the goals, standing in a position to see the puck entering the goal, and provided with small flags or white handkerchiefs.

5. He will get the captains to toss up for choice of ends.

6. He will advise the players of the rules applying to substitution, exhort them to keep calm, and inform them of the way in which penalties will be inflicted.

7. In case of bad weather the referee shall decide if the match shall be postponed ; if there are two referees the match shall not be postponed unless both are in agreement ; but a match once begun shall always be continued unless the referee (or referees) and both of the team captains agree otherwise.

(b) *During the Match.*

1. He will place the puck in play and show by blowing the whistle that play has commenced.

2. He will stop the game for any infringement and, if necessary, penalize the players at fault ; he will not, however, stop play for an infringement if the stoppage would benefit the team of the player committing same, unless the referee considers a stoppage necessary in order to penalize the player at fault and so prevent the game from becoming rough ;

3. He will inform the penalty timekeepers of the penalties inflicted ;

4. He will stop play at the scoring of each goal and decide whether the goal is valid or not (by consulting the goal umpire, though without necessarily accepting the latter's opinion).

5. After each stoppage he will put the puck in play and show by blowing his whistle that play has recommenced.

6. He will settle disputes of all kinds.

7. He will stop play if one of the players is hurt, and also in the circumstances mentioned in Art. 10.

8. He will stop play as soon as the timekeepers inform him that the period is over.

(c) *During the Rest.*

1. He will remain in communication with the timekeepers and the players, and warn the latter three minutes before the end of the rest.

2. He will ascertain whether the lines of the rink are still sufficiently clear, and if not, will have them remade.

3. He will count up the goals scored during the pre-ceeding period.

(d) *At the Resumption :*

1. He will see to it that the penalized players whose time of punishment had not expired when the rest was taken, continue their absence.

2. He will recommence the game at the correct time, even if all the players are not yet on the rink, except in the case of circumstances beyond his control.

3. He will see that the teams change ends.

4. He will referee as before.

(e) *At the end of the Match :*

He will count up the goals scored by each team in the course of the match and, if necessary, order extra time to be played.

(f) *After the Match :*

He will examine and sign the report of the match, or ' referee's sheet.' (See Appendix 5.)

ART. 55 *bis*—DOUBLE UMPIRING

(*a*) When there are two referees, each one shall in turn face off at the centre; the first referee, designated by drawing lots, shall face off during the first period and the first half of the third and of extra times; the other shall do so in the second period and the second half of the third play and of each extra time.

(*b*) One referee shall take up a position at one of the blue lines, against the railing; the other shall stay at the other blue line, against the other railing. They shall leave their positions as seldom as possible and shall return to them if obliged to move. Referees shall not change sides with the teams and shall referee during the entire game on the same blue line.

(*c*) Each referee shall be in charge of that half of the rink (between the centre and short side) where his blue line is ; he shall give all decisions required for his half of the rink. He may at any time ask the other referee's opinion, but the final decision rests with him.

(*d*) Any fouls occurring at the division of the two halves, if not agreed on by the two referees, shall be decided in the last resort by the referee in charge of the face-off during the period.

(*e*) As an exception a referee may stop play because of any foul or other incident occurring in the half of the other referee whenever such foul or incident is serious and was not noticed by the other referee. The decision and penalty, if any, shall, however, rest always with the latter.

B. THE TIMEKEEPERS

ART. 56.—Two timekeepers are appointed by the referee. They should, if possible, be neutral, but if this is not practicable, one belonging to each team should be chosen : however, if no neutral timekeepers are available, and if the two teams are unable each to appoint a time-keeper, the official timekeepers of the association in the country organizing the meeting will be appointed.

ART. 57.—Their duty is to inform the referee by blowing a whistle, ringing a bell, or beating a gong that the end of the period or of the rest has arrived.

ART. 58.—They will begin to count the time from the moment the referee blows the whistle for the first time when putting the puck into play.

ART. 59.—They will stop their watches during the stoppages of play, or, if they do not possess stop-watches, they will add to the playing time the time taken for each stoppage.

ART. 60.—They will advise the referee three minutes before the end of the interval.

ART. 61.—All disputes between them regarding the time will be settled there and then by the referee.

C. THE PENALTY TIMEKEEPERS

ART. 62.—The referee will appoint one timekeeper (if the latter is neutral, and two, one for each team, if a neutral timekeeper is not available), whose duty it is specially to keep time regarding the penalties inflicted on the players.

ART. 63.—The referee will tell them the duration of the penalty.

ART. 64.—They will commence to keep the time of the penalty only from the moment when the player sent off presents himself to them.

ART. 65.—They will add to the penalty all time lost for stoppages of play (as for the game).

ART. 66.—They will not permit the penalized player to return to play until he has completely served his sentence.

ART. 67.—When there is no stoppage of play, they will not allow another player to take the place of the penalized player at the moment that the latter is entitled to return to play.

ART. 68.—If, when the whistle goes for the rest, the player has not finished his sentence, he will finish it at the beginning of the following period. However, any penalty will be considered finished with the end of the match and will not be continued in the course of a later match.

ART. 69.—All disputes between the two penalty time-keepers will be settled forthwith by the referee.

D. THE GOAL UMPIRES

ART. 70.—The referee will appoint two goal umpires, if possible chosen from neutral persons, but if this is not practicable, one from each team.

ART. 71.—The goal umpires' duty is to inform the referee, by raising a flag or a white handkerchief, that the puck has entirely cleared the goal-line after passing over it from the front and that consequently a goal has been properly scored.

ART. 72.—This is his only duty and the only case in which he is called upon to make known his opinion; however, he must reply to the referee, if asked, as to whether in his opinion the goal has been properly scored (*i.e.* that there has been no kick, offside infringement, etc.), and shall also reply to any other question which the referee may consider it necessary to ask him.

ART. 73.—He will not change ends after the rest and will act as umpire alternately behind the goal of each team.

ART. 74.—He must place himself so as to be able to see the goal line perfectly.

ART. 75.—The referee is under no obligation to act on the judgment of the goal umpire, but shall in every case question him as to the validity of the goal scored.

IV. THE PLAY

A. Its Duration

ART. 76.—The teams will play during three periods of fifteen minutes each, separated by rests of ten minutes. Nevertheless, for matches which are not for the European or World Championships, periods may consist of twenty minutes each, if the opposing captains agree.

ART. 77.—All stoppages occurring in the game will be added to the actual playing time.

ART. 78.—If after the expiration of this time the game is undecided, *i.e.* if the two teams have each scored the same number of goals, or if neither of them has scored, extra time may be played; after a rest of ten minutes the match will be continued for ten minutes of playing time, each team playing five minutes from each end. No rest will be taken between these two periods of five minutes, but ends will be changed.

ART. 79.—If after this extra time the match is still undecided, extensions of ten minutes may be played in the same way, with a rest of five minutes between each extra time of ten minutes' duration, until a decision has been obtained.

ART. 80.—However, no match may be prolonged for more than thirty minutes of actual play, *i.e.* three periods of extra time. If after this time the match is undecided, it will be replayed.

ART. 81.—Should one of the teams refuse to play the required extra time, it will be declared to have lost.

ART. 82.—The Championships of Europe and of the World do not provide any exception to these rules.

B. WINNERS—GOALS SCORED

ART. 83.—The winning team of the match will be that which during the match, inclusive of extra time, has scored the greater number of goals.

ART. 84.—A goal is scored when the puck has entirely crossed from the front the plane formed by the goal-line, the posts, and cross-bar. The goal will not be allowed if the puck still touches the goal-line.

ART. 85.—In no case may the referee award a goal which has not thus been scored, no matter what infringement may have been committed by the defending team in preventing the goal from being scored.

ART. 86.—If, however, a goal has been scored through a foul, for instance after off-side, or through a kick, or through the goal-keeper being charged, etc., the referee will not allow the goal.

C. ENDS

ART. 87.—Before the match, in the presence of the referee, the captains of the opposing teams will toss up. The successful captain may choose the end of the rink to be defended by his team in the first period.

ART. 88.—At each new period, after seven and a half minutes of the third period, or after five minutes' extra time, the teams will change ends.

D. STOPPAGES

ART. 89.—Play will only be stopped when the referee blows his whistle.

ART. 90.—The referee will stop play

(1) when the puck has gone over the lines. The puck shall be considered as having gone out of play if it touches a spectator and rebounds on to the rink, in the same way as if it had touched the referee.

(2) when an infringement has been committed (see Art. 97) ;

(3) when the puck has touched the referee ;

(4) when a goal has been scored ;

(5) for special reasons, such as injury to a player, damage to or breakage of the goal-posts, etc. ;

(6) at the end of a period ; after seven and a half minutes of the third period ; and after five minutes of extra time.

ART. 91.—Play will not be stopped because a player has broken his stick, except when the player is the goal-keeper.

E. FACE-OFF

ART. 92.—In order to start playing the puck, two players, one from each team, will place themselves one opposite the other, at the spot indicated by the referee, the left-hand side turned towards the opposing goal and the blades of the sticks on the ice parallel and at 50 cm. (20 inches) distance from one another. The referee throws the puck between the two blades of the sticks, at the same time blowing his whistle to announce that play has begun. The players facing may not lift their sticks until the puck has touched the ice.

Art. 93.—At the face-off every player, except the two players who are facing off, shall be on-side (between the puck and the base of their zone) and at least 3 metres (10 feet) from the point of the face-off, except for the goal-keeper, who shall remain in his usual position in front of his own goal.

Art. 94.—At the beginning of a period, or when a goal has been scored, the referee faces the puck in the centre of the rink (marked by a dark circle).

Art. 95.—In the course of the game he (the referee) faces the puck at the spots hereinafter specified, according to why and where the game was stopped :—

(*a*) In the Central Zone :—

1. For off-side (*i.e.* whenever a player in the central zone received the puck from a team-mate who remained in the defence zone) : at the spot from which the puck came before the off-side.

2. For any other infringement : at the spot where the infringement was committed.

3. When the puck goes off the rink : at 3 metres (10 feet) from the long side, opposite the point where the puck left the rink.

(*b*) In the End Zones :—

A. For an infringement committed by an attacking player :—

1. For off-side (*i.e.* when a player not in possession of the puck crosses the blue line before the puck) : at the spot where the puck was when the player crossed the line.

2. For any other infringement, for an infringement committed jointly by a player from either team or because the puck went over the lines : on the blue line, at 3 metres (10 feet) from the long side nearest the spot where the infringement occurred or the puck went off,

B. For infringement by a defending player :—

1. For a minor infringement by the goal-keeper (Art. 110) and for ragging (first offence) (Art. 115) : at the spot marked on the ice in front of the goal (Art. 119) ;

2. For penalizing a defence player in excess (Art. 114) : in the centre of the rink ;

3. For any other infringement : at the spot where the infringement occurred.

ART. 96.—Nevertheless, whenever a face-off occurs in an end zone, *in front of the goal*, the point of face-off shall be carried 3 metres (10 feet) to one side of the goal at the same distance from the goal-line as the spot where the infringement occurred.

V. INFRINGEMENTS

A. GENERAL

ART. 97.—In general, the referee shall stop play for any infringement, whether intentional or not ; however, he will not stop play if such stoppage is to the advantage of the team which has committed the infringement : but if the infringement is one which calls for a penalty he will stop play *at the conclusion of that phase of the game* in order to penalize the offending player.

ART. 98.—The referee must carry out his duty sufficiently severely to maintain correct play, without, however, upsetting the players and rendering play impossible by continuous stoppages.

B. OFF-SIDE

ART. 99.—A player whose position is between the puck and his own goal is said to be ' on-side.' If he is between the puck and the opposing goal he is ' off-side.' Players of the same team shall be known as ' team-mates,' and ' opponents ' of the other team.

ART. 100.—A player may always pass the puck to a team-mate who is on-side. He may also pass it to a team-mate who is off-side, provided that this team-mate is in the same zone as himself ; he may not, however, pass the puck to a team-mate who is off-side in another zone.

ART. 101.—Nevertheless, a puck once having entered the centre zone from the defence zone may be picked up by any of the players who were in the defence zone at the moment of the pass, that is to say, they may chase the puck into the centre zone.

ART. 102.—If the puck, at the moment it passes from the defence zone into the centre zone, is played by a team-mate who was not in the defence zone at the moment when the pass was given, the game shall be stopped and a face-off shall take place at the point whence the pass originated.

(The game, however, shall not be stopped if the pass comes from the opponent who is at the time in the defence zone of the player receiving it, the defence players not being obliged to follow the puck into their defence zone.)

ART. 103.—A second defence zone is the *goal area* (Article 5 (*d*) and Appendix 6). This bears the same relation to the remainder of the rink as the defence zone itself bears to the two other zones, that is to say :—

1. That an attacking player can only enter the goal area *after* the puck has entered it, even if he is on-side.

2. That nevertheless, if an attacking player after having transgressed in entering it leaves it again before the puck enters the area the game shall not be stopped ; and finally,

3. That once *within* the goal area players who have lawfully entered it may pass to one another even in an off-side position.

ART. 104.—Even in the attacking zone, players who are off-side may join in the game provided always that they do not impede the view or interfere with the movements of the goal-keeper. In the event of any such infringement the game shall be stopped and any goal scored thereby shall be void.

To mark the portion of the rink within which off-side players may be considered likely to interfere with the goal-keeper, a special section, known as the ' goal-crease,' shall be outlined on the ice : a circle of 3 m. radius (10 feet) having as centre the middle of the goal-line and consisting of a stripe 5 cm. (2 inches) in width, shall be drawn around the goal, terminating behind it on a line running parallel with the goal-line and at a distance of 0.55 m. (22 inches) therefrom (see Appendix 6).

ART. 105.—Defending players may harass attackers, even those not in possession of the puck, but without using sticks or tackling, body checking being permitted only against players in possession of the puck.

ART. 106.—In the event of a pile-up in the goal-crease such that the referee loses sight of the puck, he shall stop the game.

C. CARRYING THE PUCK—KICKING

ART. 107.—All players may stop the puck with any part of the body ; but they must let it fall on the rink ; it is not permitted to carry the puck or to play it in any other way but with the stick, but the players shall be able to use their sticks as they like, to hit the puck, to push it with the stick or carry it on the stick, on condition that they do not raise the stick higher than their shoulder.

ART. 108.—Nevertheless, in the defence zone and the centre zone a player shall be permitted to ' foot-lag ' the puck on to his stick, but shall not be allowed to kick it or to pass it in this way to a team-mate.

D. PROHIBITED POSITIONS

ART. 109.—No player, except the goalkeeper, may lie down, sit, kneel or intentionally fall on the ice. The player who has accidentally fallen may not take part in the play and must make every effort to get up immediately.

A player who plays in one of the prohibited positions commits an infringement which is punishable should it impede a goal being scored.

ART. 110.—Only the goal-keeper or the player who replaces him while he is penalized, may stop the puck in any position (sitting, kneeling, falling) and clear it as he thinks best (kicking, throwing, etc.), with the one restriction that he may only throw it behind himself and not forward, and that he shall not hold the puck, lie, kneel or sit on it. Any minor infringement by the goal-keeper shall be penalized by the special face-off described in Art. 119.

E. CHARGING AND ROUGH PLAY

ART. 111.—All rough play is prohibited. It is particularly prohibited to charge, to trip, or to grapple with one another, to hit with the skates or sticks, or to push, hold or impede an opponent by hand

However, body checking will be allowed if carried out under the following conditions :—Cleanly, body to body, in the defence zone only, by any defence player against any attacking player *in possession of the puck* ; it can be done with the chest, the back, the shoulder or the hip, but not with the knee or elbow or with the stick pushed out in front. A player who body checks may throw his weight slightly forward towards the attacking player but without gathering momentum for the charge ; but he may not attack in the back a player who has just passed him, and body checking may not be done within five feet of the boarding.

ART. 112.—It is particularly prohibited to charge the goal-keeper while he is defending, and a goal scored under such circumstances should be declared void ; however, such defence shall be deemed lacking if the goal-keeper leaves his goal-crease.

ART. 113.—In no case may a player not playing the puck be ' body checked,' even though he may be a potential receiver of the pass.

F. Number of Players on Defence

Art. 114.—No more than three team-mates, including the goal-keeper, shall be in their defence zone when the puck is not in that zone; but where the puck has just left the defence zone, no infringement shall have been committed if the extra players leave the zone immediately the puck has done so; similarly a fourth defending player may enter his defence zone in front of the puck with the aim of impeding an opponent in possession of the puck provided he is not more than one stick's length in front of the other. For the first offence, the game shall be stopped and the puck faced off in the centre of the rink; for the second offence, the first extra player to enter his defence zone shall be penalized one minute; for the third offence, the penalty shall be two minutes, and so on, each new offence increasing the penalty by one minute. Where several extra players enter their defence zone before the puck, the captain of the offending team shall designate the player to be penalized.

G. Ragging

Art. 115.—The team which, in order to gain time, for any reason deliberately plays a defensive game, by not carrying a puck forward but circling round the same spot, carrying the puck behind the goal, etc., without any player of the offending team being in their defence zone, commits an infringement. The first offence shall be penalized by the referee facing off the puck as set out in Art. 119; for the second offence, he shall penalize the player at fault.

H. Other Infringements

Art. 116.—It is prohibited to play a ' Dirty ' or savage game, to use improper or coarse language, to have an argument with a spectator or another player, to raise the stick above the shoulder or to throw it on the ice.

ART. 117.—When the referee is of the opinion that a defending player intentionally commits a slight infringement in order to stop play at a critical moment, he will not stop play for this infringement and will penalize the player at the first stoppage following.

VI. PENALTIES

A. KINDS OF PENALTY

ART. 118.—Notwithstanding the stoppage of the game necessitating the stoppage of the puck, the referee may exclude from the game for varying periods of time a player committing an infringement, without it being permissible for the latter to be replaced during the period of his enforced absence.

ART. 119.—A special penalty shall be applied in the two cases considered under Art. 110 (minor infringement by a goal-keeper) and 115 (ragging—first offence). The referee shall face off the puck at 3 metres (10 feet) in front of, and perpendicular to, the middle of the goal of the offending team without any player of the defending team, except the goal-keeper and the player facing off, being within 5 metres (15 feet) of the nearest goal-post at the time of the face-off. A special spot shall be marked on the ice and lines painted on the boards for these distances (see Art. 5).

ART. 120.—Generally, the referee will give a warning before inflicting a penalty.

The referee will inflict penalties with the severity required to ensure a correct game free from intentional infringements. He will avoid upsetting the players by exaggerated penalties.

B. APPLICATION

ART. 121.—When in the opinion of the referee a player commits a punishable infringement, the former will, after having stopped the game, inform the player as well as the penalty timekeepers of the sentence inflicted, *i.e.* of the duration of the exclusion.

ART. 122.—The penalized player will at once leave the game and put on clothing of neutral colour.

ART. 123.—The time of the punishment will commence as soon as the game is resumed, after the sent-off player has placed himself at the disposal of the penalty time-keeper.

ART. 124.—All stoppages of play will be added to the time of punishment, which will therefore only be counted for the time actually played.

ART. 125.—As soon as the punishment is over, the penalized player (but not a substitute) will again take up his place in the game, without play being stopped. The penalty timekeeper will inform the player when his sentence is over.

ART. 126.—Such player shall skate back to his defence zone before he can again participate in the game.

ART. 127.—Should half-time arrive before the sentence has been fully served, the player will finish his sentence at the beginning of the following period ; however, in the case of a tournament, when a sentence has not been fully served by the end of the match, it will not be carried forward to the following match.

C. DURATION—SUGGESTIONS FOR PENALTIES

ART. 128.—The referee will penalize for the time thought suitable by him, one, two, five minutes, or even for the whole period if the infringement is exceptionally bad, such as intentionally causing injury to an opponent, or striking the referee.

ART. 129.—He will inflict the penalty in accordance with the importance of the infringement, its repetition, and its effect on the outcome of the game, etc.

ART. 130.—Under these circumstances it is very difficult to fix a scale of penalties ; but for guidance a few penalties may be suggested to the referees to serve as a basis, without, however, the referees being obliged to act accordingly, as the infliction of penalties is entirely subject to their judgment.

ART. 131.—Below are mentioned some penalties which might serve as an index for the referees, and these suggestions have the advantage of giving the international referees an index of a fairly equal degree of firmness :—

ONE MINUTE

To all players, except the goal-keeper, who throw the puck.

To the player who intentionally kicks the puck or pushes it with the hand or arm.

To the player holding the puck in his hand, or against the edge of the rink or any other spot along the rink by the body or foot.

To the goal-keeper who strikes an adversary with the stick or who trips him.

To the player who is intentionally off-side.

To the player who trips an opponent with the stick.

To the player who shall be in the defence zone when there are already three team-mates there (second offence).

To the player who shall ' rag ' the puck (second offence).

TWO MINUTES

To the player who unintentionally trips.

To the player who throws his stick.

To the player who throws an opponent's stick to the ground.

To the player who is intentionally off-side (repeated offence).

To the player who charges an opponent otherwise than by ' body checking.'

To the player who lifts his stick above his shoulder.

To the player who disputes with the referee.

To the player who trips with his stick (repeated offence).

To the player who argues with the spectators.

To the player who contravenes the rules relating to substitution.

THREE MINUTES

To the player who uses his stick when ' body checking.'

To the player who intentionally trips an opponent.

To the player who throws his stick in order to avoid a score.

FIVE MINUTES

To the player who injures the officials.

To the player who uses foul language.

To the player who kicks an opponent with his skate.

To the player who hits an opponent on the head with his stick.

TEN MINUTES

To the player who intentionally injures an opponent.

To the player who attacks an official.

To the player who strikes an opponent with the handle of his stick.

ICE-HOCKEY RULES CONTENTS

Plan of the Field of Play

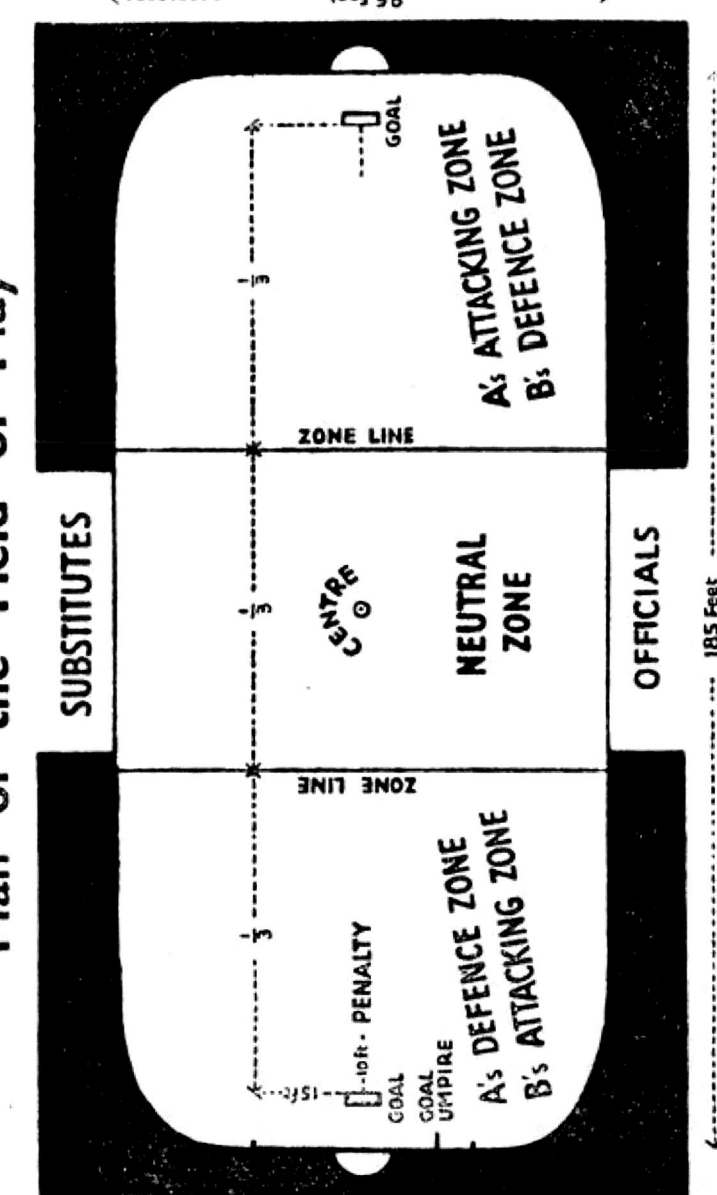

85 feet

185 Feet

SUBSTITUTES

OFFICIALS

ZONE LINE

ZONE LINE

NEUTRAL ZONE

CENTRE

A's ATTACKING ZONE
B's DEFENCE ZONE

A's DEFENCE ZONE
B's ATTACKING ZONE

GOAL

GOAL
GOAL UMPIRE

PENALTY

CHAPTER XI

THE BRITISH ICE-HOCKEY ASSOCIATION

Patrons

His Grace the Duke of Newcastle.
The Lord Decies, P.C., D.S.O.
The Lord Rochdale.
Sir Harold Bowden, Bt., G.B.E.
Major B. M. Patton (*Past President*).

Officials Past and Present

The Association was first formed in the 1913-14 season, when B. M. Patton was elected President and T. G. Cannon, Hon. Secretary and Treasurer.

Re-formed in 1923

President

1923–34.	Major B. M. Patton.
1934–36.	P. V. Hunter, C.B.E.

Hon. Secretary

1923–25.	T. G. Cannon.
1925–27.	Lt.-Col. T. Nangle.
1927–30.	Flight-Lt. V. H. Tait (Feb. 18, 1930).
1930–33.	P. V. Hunter, C.B.E., (acting) from 18/2/30.
1933–36.	J. F. Ahearne (*Secretary*).

Hon. Treasurer

1923–26. T. G. Cannon.
1926–27. Lt.-Col. T. Nangle.
1927–30. Flight-Lt. V. H. Tait (Feb. 18, 1930).
1930–36. P. V. Hunter, C.B.E., from 18/2/30.

J. C. P. Magwood was Vice-President, 1932–33 and 1933–34, and Match Secretary, 1929–30 to 1932–33, inclusive.

J. J. Justice was Assistant Secretary, 1932–33.

P. V. Hunter, C.B.E., was Vice-President, 1933–34.

C. A. Erhardt, Vice-President, 1934–35 and 1935–36.

There have formerly been other Vice-Presidents but they were not officials of the B.I.H.A.

COUNCIL OF THE B.I.H.A.

Formed October 1935

President

PHILIP VASSAR HUNTER, C.B.E., Vice-President, L.I.H.G., Past President, I.E.E.   Learned to skate and play bandy in the Fenn district of Norfolk, where he was born.   Became interested in Ice-Hockey in Switzerland after the war. Joined the old Princes I.H.C. in 1928, which had its headquarters at the Ice Club, Westminster.   Played in the Princes II team when it won the Championship of the Junior League on April 14th, 1930, and incidentally the cup he had presented to that league for competition.

Vice-President

CARL A. ERHARDT.   Joined Princes I.H.C. in 1927–28 season ; became Playing Captain in 1930 and Captain in 1931.   Next became Captain of Streatham and has filled that post up to the present.   See also in Olympic Hockey.

Members

Major W. H. MACKENZIE has been a very prominent figure in Ice-Hockey for a number of years. Formerly played for the London Lions, of which he was President for several seasons. Was an international player in 1929 and several subsequent years. This last season he had the distinction of being the oldest player in the National League, when he played for the Richmond Hawks as well as being their manager. Goes to Harringay this next season.

F. A. DE MARWICZ, has also been prominent in Ice-Hockey for a number of years. Played for London Lions and then for Streatham. Has played for England and, like W. H. Mackenzie, did a good deal of refereeing before the official referees were appointed. See also in Cambridge 'Varsity History.

G. A. STRUBBE, one of the founders of the former Hammersmith I.H.C., of which he was Hon. Secretary, a post he also filled with the Grosvenor House Canadians, 1931–32 to 1933–34. Has been manager of the Wembley Canadians for the past two seasons.

P. E. HOLMES, Cambridge. See 'Varsity History.

G. S. COWAN, Oxford. See 'Varsity History.

Secretary

J. F. AHEARNE took over this office at the beginning of the 1933–34 season and has put in a vast amount of work, with the result that the Association machinery is now in excellent running order.

CAPTAINS OF ENGLAND

1904–14	(inclusive). B. M. Patton.
1921–3.	Major B. M. Patton.
1924.	Capt. C. Carruthers, M.C.
1925.	No Captain.
1926–7.	B. N. Sexton.

1928.   Capt. C. Ross Cuthbert, M.C.
1929.   Capt. C. Ross Cuthbert, M.C., and Capt. W.
          Home, M.C.
1930.   Capt. W. Home, M.C., and J. C. P. Magwood.
1931–2.   J. C. P. Magwood.
1933.   J. C. P. Magwood and N. Melland.
1934.   N. Melland.
1935–6.   C. A. Erhardt.

CHAPTER XII

RINKS WHERE ICE-HOCKEY IS PLAYED

BIRMINGHAM ICE-SKATING RINK

Opened, September 2nd, 1931.

Ice Area, 179'×87'.
Seating Capacity, 750.   Maximum capacity, 2500.
Owners—Ice Rinks, Ltd.
Manager—James Easton, since opening.

BRIGHTON—SPORTS STADIUM

Opened, October 16th, 1935.

Ice Area, 185'×85'.
Seating Capacity, 1700.   Maximum capacity, 3000.
Special features—Open for skating in summer.   Has private and curative baths.
Owners—Sports Stadium, Brighton, Ltd.
Managing Director—C. Langdon.
Secretary—J. M. Bailly.
Rink Manager—D. Mitchell (late of the Queen's Ice Club, London).

EARL'S COURT

Opened, October 26th, 1935.

Ice Area, 200'×97'.   Seating capacity, 7100.
Special features—Very fine Press box.   Good view of arena from the corners as they are rounded off instead of being rectangular.
Managing Director—F. L. Summerhayes, who achieved great success with his team, the Grosvenor House Canadians, 1930–31 to 1933–34.   Has foreseen the great necessity to develop home talent and started junior hockey within a month from the opening of the rink.

MANCHESTER ICE PALACE

Opened, October 25th, 1910.
Closed, 1915.
Reopened, November 21st, 1919.
Ice Area, 140′ × 100′.
Seating capacity, 1100.   Maximum capacity, 2500.
Special feature—Silver Jubilee Celebration, March 28–30, 1936.
Owners—Public Company.
Chairman of Directors—A. Darbyshire, J.P.
Manager and Secretary—B. E. Wake, since 1910.   To have been ' at the helm ' during the whole period of the rink's existence speaks volumes for the efficiency of its ' Skipper.'

RICHMOND SPORTS DROME

Opened as Richmond Ice Rink, December 18th, 1928.
Ice Area, 286′ × 85′.
Closed in 1932.
Reopened, September 22nd, 1934.
Ice Area, 210′ × 85′.
Seating capacity, 2000.   Maximum capacity, 2200.
Special features—Open for skating during summer months.   Swimming pool and sun bathing (summer).
Owners—Sports Drome, Ltd.
Chairman of Directors—Major G. H. Barrington Chance.
Managing Director—C. L. Langdon.
Manager and Secretary—R. M. Marians, who previously filled same post at the Ice Drome, Hammersmith.

STREATHAM

Opened, February, 1931.
Ice Area, 210′ × 100′.
Seating capacity, 1500.   Maximum capacity, 3000.
Special feature—Very special form of floodlighting.
Owners—Privately owned.
Manager—Dunbar Poole (who has a very efficient sub-manager, R. J. Buck) has travelled the world over

and turned his hand successfully to many things. An expert figure-skater, and though born in Belfast has had the unique experience of skating in the World Amateur Figure-Skating Championship for Sweden in 1911 at Berlin. Opened up the Sydney and Melbourne rinks. Started Association football in Australia.

WEMBLEY—THE EMPIRE POOL

Opened, July 25th, 1934, for the Empire Games swimming events.

Opened for Ice-Hockey, October 25th, 1934.

Ice Area, 200′×85′.

Seating capacity, 10,000.

Special features—Thoroughly up to date, especially as regards medical appliances, such as electric heating pad for bruises, ultra-violet rays, sun-lamp treatment. Various types of foam baths. Facilities for immediate operations for serious injuries.

Owners—Wembley Stadium, Ltd.

Chairman of Directors—Major-Gen. The Rt. Hon. Lord Mottistone, C.B., C.M.G., D.S.O.

Managing Director—A. J. Elvin, who, from the 'ashes' of Wembley Exhibition, created the Stadium and the Empire Pool, which have deservedly achieved great success as the results of his hard work and great organizing powers; foresight combined with courage caused him to launch out and put Ice-Hockey 'on the map' in a big way.

Manager Paul Herbert, who is so able an 'adjutant' to the Managing Director, is one of the highest authorities on diving. He was the founder of the Highgate Diving Club, and has written a text-book on diving.

GLASGOW

Opened, 1907—Closed, 1918.

Reopened, 1929.

Ice Area, 225′×97′ (whole area used for hockey).

Seating capacity, 2600. Maximum capacity, 3000.

Owners—Scottish Ice Rink Company (1928), Ltd.

Chairman of Directors—Frank Stuart.

Manager—James Gourley.

NEW RINKS

HARRINGAY

To open, October 5th, 1936.
Ice Area, 184'×89'.   Seating capacity, 9000.
Owners—Harringay, Ltd.
Secretary—A. Whatley.

PERTH

In course of construction.
Ice surface, 185'×85'.
Seating for 2500.
Will have six hockey teams.

See also last paragraph, Scottish Ice-Hockey.

CHAPTER XIII

CLUBS AFFILIATED TO THE B.I.H.A.

Brighton Tigers

Formed, September 1935.

Vice-Presidents—The Earl Howe ; The Lord St. Oswald ; Sir Harry Preston (the late).

Chairman—B. S. Cannell.

Captain—L. Sargent.

Vice-Captain—R. Beaton.

Secretary—H. A. West, Rokeby, Miller's Road, Brighton.

Number of Members—20.

Colours—Jersey and stockings, black and yellow stripes ; shorts, blue.

Badge—Tiger's head.

Match days—Thursdays.

League and Cup Competitions—N.L.

Distinguished players—R. Beaton, a distinguished Canadian boxer ; J. S. Borland, Member British Olympic team 1936.

Coach—E. P. Nicklin.   Trainer—N. Clarke.

Earl's Court Rangers

Formed, October 25th, 1935.

President—A. F. Currie.

Captain—R. McAlpine.

Vice-Captain—D. Hodges.

Secretary—Don Wilson.

Abbreviations :—N.L.—National League. E.L.—English League. L.P.C.T.—London-Paris Club Tournament. L.C.—London Cup. C.C.—Channel Cup. E.S.C.—Empress Stadium Cup.

Number of Members—12.

Colours—Jersey and stockings, orange and brown ; shorts, brown.

Badge—Rangers.

Match days—Fridays.

League and Cup Competitions—N.L., L.P.C.T., C.C., L.C., E.S.C.

Distinguished players—J. Chappell, member of British Olympic team 1936. Frank Currie is a motor-cycling ace in Canada. P. MacPhail and R. McAlpine played for Scotland this last season. Had the latter not been a member of the Canadian team that took part in the World Championship at Prague in 1933, he would in all probability have been a member of our Olympic team this year, as he is Scottish born.

Coach—Joe Smith. Trainer—James Taylor.

Joe Smith, for the two or three seasons previous to coming over here to take charge of the Rangers, searched all Canada for youthful talent for the New York Rangers, which he coached in ' Farms ' around New York. Incidentally, Joe Smith was manager of Ernest Leacock's first professional club, the Victoria Cubs, in 1927–28 season in the Pacific Coast League.

Club's Achievements—Scored more goals in N.L. matches than any other team.

KENSINGTON CORINTHIANS

Formed, October 25th, 1935.

President—Beacher Moore.

Captain—J. E. Brown.

Secretary—J. Riddell.

Number of Members—13.

Colours—Jersey and stockings, blue and white ; Shorts, blue.

Badge—K.C.

Match days—Mondays.

League and Cup Competitions—N.L., L.P.C.T., C.C., L.C. and E.S.C.

Distinguished Players—J. E. Brown, member of the

Edmonton Superiors that visited England and Europe, 1932. E. Yates, star bicycle rider, rode for Canada in Olympic Games at Los Angeles, 1932.

Coach—F. Towell. Trainer, W. Brown.

Fred Towell was a very good amateur player and played in the same team as Ernest Leacock in Portland, Oregon, in 1927. He also played in Calgary, Alberta, in different clubs and later was coach.

Club's Achievements—Winners of E.S.C. and runners-up for C.C.

Richmond Hawks

Formed, September 1914.

President—W. B. Milford.

Vice-President—Major Barington Chance.

Captain—Joe Beaton

Vice-Captain—Neville Melland.

Secretary and Manager—Major W. H. Mackenzie,[1] Royal Air Force Club, Piccadilly.

Number of Members—12.

Colours—Jersey and stockings, white with black stripes ; shorts, dark blue.

Badge—Black Hawk.

Match Days—Tuesdays.

League and Cup Competitions—N.L., L.P.C.T., C.C., L.C.

Distinguished Players—N. Melland, International 1926. 1928 Olympic team and 1930 to 1934. Captain of National teams part 1933 and for 1934. Oxford Lacrosse ' Blue.' Played for Oxford 1923–26. President and Captain 1925–26. Captain Oxford–Cambridge team which toured U.S.A. 1926. Played for Lancashire and for South v. North several times. Distinguished also at lawn tennis.

Joe Beaton is a noted boxer.

Coach—P. H. Nicklin. Trainer—N. Clarke.

Percy Nicklin, who coached our Olympic team so successfully this year, collected material which formed the Moncton Hawks teams of 1932–34 and which won the Allan Cup the latter two years.

[1] Goes to Harringay, is replaced by G. A. Strubbe late of Wembley Canadians.

Club's Achievements—Runners-up N.L. Championship, lost on goal average only. Lost fewer matches than any other team in the N.L.

STREATHAM

Formed, September 1933.

President—Stanley Brown.

Vice-Presidents—Major B. M. Patton; P. V. Hunter, C.B.E.; E. Ramus, Sr.

Captain—C. A. Erhardt.

Vice-Captain—H. Stapleford.

Secretary—E. J. Ramus, Jr., 4 Holmwood House, 75 Anson Road, N.7.

Number of Members—31

Colours—Jersey and stockings, red, white and blue; shorts, dark blue.

Badge—Gold skate in circle, 'Streatham Ice-Hockey Club' written above and below two vertical hockey sticks outside with puck.

Match Days—Wednesdays; Fridays occasionally.

League and Cup Competitions—N.L., E.L., L.P.C.T., L.C.

Distinguished Players—C. A. Erhardt, Captain British Olympic team 1936 and National team 1935; International 1931–32–33–34, also a very noted lawn tennis player. Baron H. Trauttenberg, Captain of Austrian National team 1931–36 inclusive; Captain of Cambridge 1931. G. Davey, British Olympic team 1936; International, 1932–33–34–35. A. Stinchcombe, British Olympic team 1936 and, with H. Stapleford, was member of Windsor Mic-Macs, winners of Michigan, Ontario, Hockey League 1933–34. R. W. Couldrey, 1933, and E. Ramus, 1933, Internationals. G. Shaw, celebrated sprinter, has defeated Pearson of the 1932 Canadian Olympic team; run 100 in 9 9/10. P. Halford, winner of many cups for rowing. P. M. Davis, like C. A. Erhardt, noted lawn tennis player. M. Gerth, like P. Halford, G. Shaw and H. Stapleford, distinguished at baseball.

Coach—J. J. Donnelly. Trainer—G. Bourner.

J. J. Donnelly played left defence for Soo in 1923, when his team won the N.O.A.H. Senior Championship.

Club's Achievements—Runners-up in the L.P.T.C. and the L.C. ; third in N.L., in which fewer goals were scored against the club than any other in the League.

WEMBLEY CANADIANS

Formed, September 6th, 1934.

President—Sir George McLaren Brown.

Chairman—Herbert Mills.

Vice-Chairman, C. Mayer.

Captain—J. G. Carr.

Vice-Captain—G. McWilliams.

Secretary—G. A. Strubbe, 109 Jermyn Street, S.W.1.

Colours—Jersey, red ; stockings, white ; shorts, green.

Badge—Green Maple Leaf.

Match Days—Saturdays.

League and Cup Competitions—N.L., L.P.C.T., L.C., C.C.

Distinguished Players—' Jimmy ' Carr was Captain of Cambridge 1934. He had to leave for Egypt just before the end of the season. He will be a great loss to hockey in 1936–37. R. Wyman, member of British Olympic team 1936 ; International 1934–35 ; holds British amateur quarter-mile speed-skating and has won several other British Championships ; winner of numerous cups for running, jumping, swimming and diving. C. Rost, noted lacrosse player. W. Cunningham and J. H. Milford, at baseball.

Coach—C. Benedict. Trainer—Ted Husbands.

Clinton Benedict has been in four Stanley Cup teams as goal-keeper. In 1923 his team, the Ottawa Senators, won the Stanley Cup and the Championship of the N.J.L. He has been in professional hockey for eighteen years.

Club's Achievements—Winners of C.C.

WEMBLEY LIONS

Formed, March 26th, 1934.

President—Sir Noel Curtis-Bennett, K.C.V.O.

Vice-Presidents—Major B. M. Patton ; P. V. Hunter, C.B.E.

Chairman—Major H. B. Cook, M.C.

Captain—Lou Bates ; also coach.

Secretary—E. C. Pitt, 31 Mayfields, Wembley Park.

Team Manager—E. Jackson.

Number of Members—12.

Colours—Jersey, white with red and white arms ; shorts, red ; stockings, red and white.

Badge—Lion as specially designed for the British Empire Exhibition of 1925.

Match Days—Thursdays.

League and Cup Competitions—N.L., L.C., C.C.

Distinguished Players—Lou Bates has represented Canada as a Canadian canoeist ; Captain of Ottawa All-stars that visited England in 1931 ; an all-round athlete, and was voted the best in Ottawa in 1932. G. Dailley, International 1933–34–35, and member of British Olympic team 1936. A. Archer and J. Kilpatrick, also members of British Olympic team 1936 ; the former a very noted ' soccer ' player in Western Canada, and the latter the youngest of our Olympic players.

Club's Achievements—Winners of N.L. and L.P.C.T.

Birmingham Maple Leafs

Formed, September 6th, 1935.

President—A. D. Kelso.

Vice-Presidents—C. A. Corwin ; D. Swincler ; J. B. Creese-Parsons.

Captain—Basil Tennier.

Secretary, Manager and Coach—S. Bissett, 20 Priory Road, Edgbaston.

Trainer—T. Jones.

Number of Members—12.

Colours—Jersey, white and black ; shorts, black with white side stripes ; stockings, white with three black rings.

Badge—Black Maple Leaf surmounted with ' Birmingham Maple Leafs.'

Match Days—Saturdays and Thursdays.

League and Cup Competitions—E.L.

F 2

Distinguished Players—H. Smith, member Saskatoon Quakers, toured Europe 1934. S. Bissett, International Baseball pitcher. T. Kennedy, Australian Speed-Skating Champion 1931–32–33–34 ; British indoor half-mile and mile ditto 1935.

Club's Achievements—Winner of English League.

Results of all Matches :—

	Played	Won	Drawn	Lost	Goals for	Goals against
League .	10	10	0	0	109	19
Exhibition .	28	15	4	9	129	99
Total	38	25	4	9	238	118

MANCHESTER

Formed, as Lancashire, 1910, and Manchester, 1912.
President—A. Darbyshire, J.P.
Captain—Gordon Johnson.
Vice-Captain—D. C. Gattiker.
Secretary—Noel Edwards, Manchester Ice Palace.
Number of Members—30.
Colours—Jersey and stockings, orange ; shorts, blue.
Match Days—Wednesdays, Thursdays, Sundays.
Distinguished Players—Gordon Johnson was Captain of Oxford in 1932–33. D. C. Gattiker was Captain of Cambridge in 1932–33.

STREATHAM ROYALS

Played	Won	Lost	Drawn	Goals for	Goals against
9	5	2	2	56	30

Awarded three other games on default.

SUSSEX

Formed, January 1930.
Non-active, 1932–34.
Re-formed, October 1935.

Vice-Presidents—The Earl Howe ; The Lord St. Oswald ; Sir Harry Preston (the late).

Captain—W. B. Trethewey.

Chairman—B. S. Cannell.

Secretary—H. A. West, Rokeby, Miller's Road, Brighton.

Number of Members—15.

Colours—Jersey, white with blue band ; shorts, blue ; stockings, blue with white band.

Badge—Copy of Sussex County Badge over skates and crossed hockey sticks.

Match Days—Alternate Mondays.

Friendly matches only played.

Marlborough Ice-Hockey Club

Formed, November 11th, 1935.

Captain—Lloyd Mills.

Junior Captain—R. G. Willson.

Secretary and Treasurer—W. A. S. How, 25 Park Lane, W.1.

Number of Members—30.

Colours—Jersey, white, diagonal blue sash, blue cuffs ; shorts, blue ; stockings, blue and white stripes.

Badge—Large blue M. surmounted by coronet in gold.

Matches Played—Friendlies. Results :—

Won 3. Drn 2. Lost 5. Goals for, 42. Goals agst., 72.

NOTE.—The badge is not for general wear ; will be very difficult to obtain as it will only be awarded to players who display very great keenness combined with exceptionally improved form.

Headquarters—Empress Stadium.

St. Thomas's Hospital

Formed, November 13th, 1935.

President—C. Max Page, F.R.C.S.

Captain—H. F. Moseley.

Secretary—J. H. Stayter.

Treasurer—H. E. de Wardener.

Number of Members—20.

Colours—Jersey, shorts and stockings, navy blue.

Badge—White skull over crossed hockey sticks, 'St. Thomas's' below.

Matches Played—Friendlies.

Won 4. Drn. 1. Lost 2. Goals for, 10. Goals agst., 11.

St. Thomas's 'A' met Guy's 'A' twice, won 5—2 and drew 1—1.

Headquarters—Empress Stadium.

United Hospitals

Composed of players from Guy's, St. George's, St. Thomas's and University; played three friendlies.

Won 1. Lost 2. Goals for, 10. Goals against, 11.

Headquarters—Empress Stadium.

Scottish I.H. Association

Formed, 1929.

President—Frank Stuart.

Vice-President—Andrew Mitchell.

Secretary—J. R. Gilmour, c/o Scottish Ice Rink, Tetwood Road, Glasgow, S.

Coach—G. Fraser. Trainer.—A. Robertson.

Colours—Jersey, white, red bands, black lion rampant ; shorts, blue ; stockings, white and red.

Match Days—Tuesdays and Fridays.

Distinguished Players — W. Fullerton has held the Scottish Amateur Speed-Skating Championship since January 1933, and is British Indoor Mile Champion. W. S. McLeod, Scottish Golf International.

Princes

Affiliated but non-active

Formed, December 23rd, 1896 (probable date).

First practice, January 4th, 1897.

Pre-1914–15.   President—The Duchess of Bedford.

,,   ,,   Captain—B. M. Patton.

,,   ,,   Hon. Secretary and Treasurer—T. G. Cannon.

Re-formed, October 19th, 1926
President—1926–29, The Duchess of Bedford.
       ,,   1930–33, T. G. Cannon.
Vice-Presidents—1931–33, Major B. M. Patton ; P. V.
                                    Hunter, C.B.E.
Hon. Treasurer—1926–33, T. G. Cannon.
Captain   —1926–30, Major B. M. Patton.
Vice-Captain   —Brig.-General Critchley, C.M.G.,
                              D.S.O.
Vice-Captain   —1929–30, C. A. Erhardt.
Captain   —1931–32, C. A. Erhardt.

On 12th November 1932, Princes merged with Queens and were called 'The P's and Q's,' except for occasional matches.

Became non-active after 1933.

Distinguished Players—B. J. T. Bosanquet, 1898 ; a very famous cricketer, played for Eton, Oxford, Middlesex and all England ; gained a great reputation as the ' Googly ' bowler. J. J. Cawthra, 1902 ; famous athlete ; founder of the Inter-'Varsity match (see 'Varsity Hockey). G. E. Clarkson, 1914; played for Toronto University (inter-collegiate senior champions, 1913) (referred to in History and Olympic chapters). Brig.-Gen. Critchley, C.M.G., D.S.O., 1926 ; a very noted golf player ; introduced Dog Racing to this country. C. A. Erhardt, 1927 ; Captain of British Olympic team, 1936 (see History and Olympic chapters). Captain Nigel Haig, 1902 ; a most distinguished long period ; racquets, tennis player and cricketer ; captained Middlesex for several years. Percy Lambert, 1909 ; a noted racing motorist, killed while racing at Brooklands, 1911. A. Noel Macklin, 1902 ; another noted Brooklands early-day racer. Col. J. T. C. Moore-Brabazon, M.C., M.P., 1909, 1926 (see History chapter) ; aviator and motorist of the very earliest days, when he won big events in both sports ; was the first Englishman to fly in this country, and holds the Royal Aero Club's No. 1 Certificate. Vane Pennell, 1897 ; one of the very finest racquet players of his day ; kept his form for an exceptional number of years. Ivan Snell, 1909 ; a famous ' Corinthian ' goal-keeper ; now a distinguished London police - court magistrate.

T. O. M. Sopwith, who is known, of course, the world over as the owner of various big-class yachts and his races in ' Endeavour I ' for the America Cup ; in 1910 was goal-keeper to the English team when it won the European Championship for the first time ; also a famous early-day aviator and won the De Forest prize for the longest flight from England to abroad, about 144 miles. E. Thornton-Smith, 1909, 1926 ; a prominent race - horse owner, in addition to many other activities. Howard Webster, 1914 ; was, like G. E. Clarkson, a member of the 1913 Toronto University team.

The year given after players' names is the year they joined the club.

New Clubs Formed in 1936

Earl's Court Rangers at the Empress Stadium (in place of the Kensington Corinthians).

Wembley Monarchs (in place of Wembley Canadians).

Harringay Greyhounds and Harringay Racers at Harringay.

CHAPTER XIV

ENGLISH CLUB CHAMPIONS

1898. Niagara.

1899. Princes.

1900. Princes.

1901. Princes.

1902. Cambridge.

1903. London Canadians.

1904. London Canadians.

1905. Princes.

1906. Princes.

1907. Oxford Canadians.

1908. Princes.

1909. Princes.

1910. Oxford Canadians.

1911. Oxford Canadians.

1912. Princes (unchallenged).

1913. Oxford Canadians.

1914. Princes.

1928. United Services.

1929. United Services.

1930. London Lions.

1931. London Lions.

1932. Oxford.

1933. Oxford.

1934. Grosvenor House Canadians.

1935. Streatham.

1936. Wembley Lions.

CUP WINNERS

INTERNATIONAL CLUB TOURNAMENT

(Title changed to London-Paris Club Tournament, 1935)

1935. Streatham.

1936. Wembley Lions.

LONDON CUP

1935. Wembley Canadians.

1936. Earl's Court Rangers.

CHANNEL CUP

1935. Wembley Canadians.

1936. Wembley Lions.

143

WINNERS OF ENGLISH LEAGUE, 1936
Birmingham Maple Leafs

LEAGUE AND CUP TABLES, 1935-36

NATIONAL LEAGUE TABLE

	P.	W.	D.	L.	Goals F.	A.	Pts.
Wembley Lions . .	24	15	3	6	96	54	33
Richmond Hawks . .	24	14	5	5	83	52	33
Streatham . . .	24	14	4	6	68	50	32
Wembley Canadians .	24	14	2	8	59	57	30
Earl's Court Rangers .	24	10	4	10	98	68	24
Brighton Tigers . .	24	3	3	18	49	98	9
Kensington Corinthians .	24	2	3	19	64	138	7

LONDON CUP

	P.	W.	D.	L.	Goals F.	A.	Pts.
Earl's Court Rangers .	10	7	1	2	40	26	15
Streatham . . .	10	6	1	3	54	49	13
Wembley Lions .	9	5	1	3	42	37	11
Wembley Canadians .	8	3	1	4	17	26	7
Richmond Hawks .	9	1	2	6	37	34	4
Kensington Corinthians .	8	2	0	6	39	57	4

LONDON-PARIS CLUB TOURNAMENT

FINAL POSITIONS—POOL A

	P.	W.	D.	L.	Goals F.	A.	Pts.
Wembley Lions .	12	6	3	3	44	36	15
Français Volants .	12	6	3	3	35	27	15
Richmond Hawks . .	12	5	4	3	42	25	14
Kensington Corinthians .	12	1	2	9	41	73	4

FINAL POSITIONS—POOL B

	P.	W.	D.	L.	Goals F.	A.	Pts.
Stade Français	12	5	5	2	29	24	15
Streatham	12	5	4	3	42	39	14
Earl's Court Rangers	12	5	3	4	39	37	13
Wembley Canadians	12	2	2	8	32	42	6

INTERNATIONAL CUP

SEMI-FINAL PLAY-OFFS

	P.	W.	D.	L.	Goals F.	A.
Streatham	2	2	0	0	9	5
Français Volants	2	0	0	2	5	9
Wembley Lions	3	2	0	1	5	3
Stade Français	3	1	0	2	3	5

CHANNEL CUP

SEMI-FINAL PLAY-OFFS

	P.	W.	D.	L.	Goals F.	A.
Wembley Canadians	2	2	0	0	3	3
Richmond Hawks	2	0	0	2	3	3

Wembley Canadians, after losing at Wembley, were awarded the match as Richmond Hawks did not play a properly qualified team.

	P.	W.	D.	L.	Goals F.	A.
Kensington Corinthians	3	2	0	1	18	15
Earl's Court Rangers	3	1	0	2	15	18

FINAL

	P.	W.	L.	Goals F.	A.
Wembley Lions . . .	2	2	0	6	3
Streatham	2	0	2	3	6

FINAL

	P.	W.	L.	Goals F.	A.
Wembley Canadians . .	2	2	0	21	5
Kensington Corinthians .	2	0	2	5	21

. WINNERS OF OLYMPIC HONOURS

AND

WINNERS OF THE WORLD AND EUROPEAN CHAMPIONSHIPS

WINNERS OF OLYMPIC HONOURS

Year.	Country.	Place.	Number of countries who competed.	Gt. Britain's position.
1920.	Canada.	Antwerp	Seven	Absent.
1924.	Canada.	Chamonix.	Eight.	Third.[1]

[1] (Defeated all European countries.)

Year.	Country.	Place.	Number of countries who competed.	Gt. Britain's position.
1928.	Canada.	St. Moritz.	Eleven.	Fourth.
1932.	Canada.	Lake Placid.	Four.	Absent.
1936.	England.	{Garmisch Partenkirchen.}	Fifteen.	First.

Schedule of Results :—

Canada.   Four wins.
England.   One win.

WINNERS OF THE WORLD CHAMPIONSHIP

Year.	Country.	Place.	Number of countries who competed.	Gt. Britain's position.
1924.	Canada.	Chamonix.	Eight.	Third.
1928.	Canada.	St. Moritz.	Eleven.	Fourth.
1930.	Canada.	Chamonix and Berlin.	Twelve.	Unplaced.
1931.	Canada.	Krynica.	Ten.	Eighth.
1932.	Canada.	Lake Placid.	Four.	Absent.
1933.	U.S.A.	Prague.	Twelve.	Absent.
1934.	Canada.	Milan.	Twelve.	Eighth.
1935.	Canada.	Davos.	Fifteen.	Third.
1936.	England.	Garmisch Partenkirchen.	Fifteen.	First.

Schedule of Results :—

Canada.　　Seven wins.

England. ⎫
U.S.A. 　⎭ One win each.

WINNERS OF EUROPEAN CHAMPIONSHIP

Year.	Country.	Place.	Number of countries who competed.	Gt. Britain's position.
1910.	England.	Les Avants.	Four.	First.
1911.	Bohemia.	Berlin.	—	Absent.
1912.		Prague.	—	Absent.

(Annulled by the Congress at Brussels.)

1913.	Belgium.	Munich.	Four.	Absent.
1914.	Bohemia.	Berlin.	—	Absent.
1921.	Sweden.	Stockholm.	Two.	Absent.
1922.	Czecho-slovakia.	St. Moritz.	Three.	Absent.

Year.	Country	Place.	Number of countries who competed.	Gt. Britain's position.
1923.	Sweden.	Antwerp.	Five.	Absent.
1924.	France.	Milan.	Six.	Absent.
1925.	{ Czecho-slovakia. }	Prague.	Four.	Absent.
1926.	{ Switzer-land. }	Davos.	Nine.	Fourth.
1927.	Austria.	Vienna.	Six.	Absent.
1928.	Sweden.	St. Moritz.	Ten.	Third.
1929.	{ Czecho-slovakia. }	Budapest.	Eight.	Absent.
1930.	Germany.	{ Chamonix and Berlin. }	Ten.	Retired.

(Ice failed at Chamonix, so finals played in Berlin.)

Year.	Country	Place.	Number of countries who competed.	Gt. Britain's position.
1931.	Austria.	{ Krynica (Poland). }	Eight.	Sixth.
1932.	Sweden.	Berlin.	Nine.	Seventh.
1933.	{ Czecho-slovakia. }	Prague.	Ten.	Absent.
1934.	Germany.	Milan.	Ten.	Sixth.
1935.	{ Switzer-land. }	Davos.	Fourteen.	Second.
1936.	England.	{ Garmisch-Partenkirchen. }	Twelve.	First.

Schedule of Results :—

Czechoslovakia	.	Six wins.
Sweden	. .	Four wins.
Austria	. .	
England	. .	
Germany	. .	Two wins each.
Switzerland	. .	
Belgium	. .	
France	. .	One win each.
Other countries	.	None.

CHAPTER XV

THE OFFICIAL REFEREES OF 1935-36
WITH SHORT BIOGRAPHIES OF EACH

JAMES FOLEY was at St. Mary's College, Halifax, where there was a special class for coaches. He went straight to coach Lunenburg in 1930, which reached the finals in North Canada for the first time. He was at that time the youngest coach in Canada. Two seasons ago he played with and coached the Milan team.

D. GEE played amateur hockey in and around Stratford, Ontario. He was goal-keeper for Birmingham two seasons ago.

' SAILOR ' HERBERTS has been a crack professional player. Was a member of the famous National (professional) League team, the Boston Bruins, a few years back. Has also played in minor professional leagues in Canada and the U.S.A.

ERNEST LEACOCK was born in London but has lived mostly in Canada. Played amateur for Banff, Alberta and Portland, Oregon, U.S.A. Later turned professional with Victoria, B.C., where he played two seasons in Pacific Coast League. Next season with Tarema in same league ; the following season with Saskatoon, Saskatchewan, in the North-Western Pro. League, and then two seasons with Portland in the same league.

G. SHOULDIS, an old player of the ' old school,' played for Ottawa and other cities in Eastern Canada with some of the ' stars ' of the time.

CHAPTER XVI

MODERN-DAY PLAY AND COMPARISON BETWEEN THE PRESENT AND THE PAST, MENTIONING ALSO CERTAIN CHANGES IN PLAY AND RULES, WITH THOSE RESPONSIBLE FOR THEM

In comparing present-day play with that of the past, P. H. Nicklin, coach to the successful British Olympic team, says that, " like the automobile and all machinery, present-day play has improved ; a first-class team is a machine, fast and scientific.

" In the old days of the game every man played for himself, often two or three men chasing the puck and scrambling in the corners.

" To-day's game is like a prize fight ; ' sparring for openings ' and trying to get the other team to make mistakes. Mistakes make the game ; if two teams played perfect hockey, the puck would remain in the centre ice."

A very notable example of ' sparring for openings ' was witnessed on April 11th last at Wembley during the first period of a vital National League match between Wembley Lions and Richmond Hawks. Percy Nicklin, it will be remembered, was coach to the Hawks last season, and had given his comments to the author about ten days previous to this match. During the 1936-37 season, with more high-class teams in action, there will of course be numerous examples to illustrate Mr. Nicklin's remarks.

One old-time method of play both in Canada and here was swept away by Lester Patrick, who with his brother are referred to a little further on. Defence players never went up the ice ; they merely lifted the puck to somewhere near their opponents' goal on the chance that one of their forwards might bang it in. One day, Lester, a defence player, who was a good stick handler and fast skater, broke a sacred tradition and recognized convention ! He took the puck up the rink and through the opposing defence up to the goal. Altercation with team-manager McWinter was the result of this daring deed. Lester argued that why should the defence throw the puck up the ice for the other side to see what they could do with it ? Eventually Lester was allowed to go ahead with his ' crazy notion.' McWinter added, however, that if the opposing side got through and scored while cover-point was away up the ice playing ' Cops and Robbers ' in his opponents' territory, it was going to be too bad ! As cover-point has been mentioned it is opportune to mention the composition of teams thirty years ago and over. Teams were of seven, and their positions on the ice were as set out below :—

o   o   o

Forwards.

o

Rover.

o

Cover-Point.

o

Point.

o

Goal-keeper.

Rinks in Canada were much smaller in the early days, but in the late 'nineties a rule was passed laying down that rinks must be at least 112 feet long by 58 feet wide. What congestion there must have been. We even found that so at Princes when we played seven a side ; which rink was as long as 210 feet but only 52 feet wide.

Referring back to Lester Patrick's innovation, it was

successfully worked in many matches, with the result
that it became firmly established. Present-day hockey
spectators who have been to Wembley have seen an excellent example in Lou Bates, a defence player and captain
of the Wembley Lions for the past two seasons. This
player frequently takes the puck down the rink, to the
delight of his club's enthusiastic supporters, to their accompanying call of L-O-U, L-O-U. The uninitiated, until they
had learned to the contrary, thought that he was un-
popular and that the spectators were ' Booing ' not
' Louing ' !

And now to explain why play of the present day is so
much faster than it was formerly and consequently, of
course, far more attractive to watch.

Various alterations in the rules from time to time are
the causes of this great ' speeding-up.'

Without zones in all three of which forward passing is
permitted, or kicking if only in two, and without substitutes
except in case of injury, how could a really fast game be
played ? How could the same three forwards keep up
great speed to attack as well as return to help the defence
for three full periods of twenty minutes each, with possibly
as much as thirty minutes over time ?

It was only during the past season that forward passing
was permitted, in Europe, in all three zones as compared
with two in the previous season ; a very great improvement,
of course.

As a result of this forward passing in all three zones
' a new move ' in the game developed over here this past
season. A forward, usually the centre, having got as far
as his opponents' defence, would often endeavour to pass
the puck between them to another forward on his side who
had skated to a position behind the defence and as much
as possible between them and the goal. It also occasionally
happened that a forward having passed the puck between
the opposing defence would try the dangerous tactic of
trying to skate between them. Very rarely did this come
off, and in a match at Earl's Court a ' star ' player got laid
out for some time in endeavouring to break through and
get the puck again.

The only differences now between the European rules and those of North America are that over there

(1) Playing the puck after a fall is permitted.
(2) Kicking takes place in all three zones.

When we adopt these two rules we shall have an improved game. If ever we have three lines of forwards, as there are in Canada in professional hockey, the game will of course be faster still.

Canada is the home of Ice-Hockey as England is of cricket. If the rules of the latter game are adopted *en bloc* by Australia, New Zealand, South Africa and Canada, who sent us a team this past summer, why should not the last-named country's Ice-Hockey rules be also adopted *en bloc*. One advantage of having the rules of the game on both sides of the Atlantic the same would be this. Players of North American teams would not have to get accustomed to what can be done and what cannot be done over here ; they would be saved from making unintentional infringements of our rules.

Earlier in this chapter reference was made to Lester Patrick, regarding the bold and successful innovation in play that he was responsible for. Further and very great credit is due to him and also his brother Frank for having introduced numerous changes in hockey rules and customs. It is said that the brothers are responsible for the introduction for as large an amount as a score in the change of rules, whereby the game has greatly benefited.

The most important changes they caused to be brought in are :—

The creation of the three-zone system.
Permitting the goal-keeper to lie and to throw the puck
    anywhere except forward.
Additional substitutes.
Kicking within reasonable limits.

Also, they introduced the modern system of granting an 'assist' to the one or more play-makers who were the means of a goal being scored, thus making the goal-getter share the credit with whoever made the goal possible. By this method team-play was built up much easier, and selfish individual players, ' stars ' or otherwise, discountenanced.

Mr. Frank Patrick, like his brother, was a famous player also. He has been coach to the Boston Bruins for two years, while Lester is director of hockey at Madison Square Gardens and coach to the New York Rangers.

CHAPTER XVII

COACHING AND TRAINING AND TEAM
MANAGERS' DUTIES

IN the multitude of counsellors there is wisdom, but it is very doubtful if any manager who is coach as well applies identical methods of coaching and training.

No single set of rules can apply to the training and coaching of any athletic organization, owing to the difference of classification of sports as well as to the characteristics of athletes ; such things, however, as physical qualities, co-ordination of mind and muscle, and, in a collective sport such as Ice-Hockey, team play, embody the underlying principle.

The problems of coaching and training are supposed to be manifold, but some doubt if they really are so. Joe Smith says that the main thing in coaching a team is common sense. The training and coaching, including study of individual members, is very necessary and takes time, says Percy Nicklin, who so successfully coached our Olympic team.

It has often been said that a manager or coach will not be of much use because he has had no experience as a professional hockey player. This is quite wrong, because here we have Joe Smith, who comes in this category as on the other side of the Atlantic does C. M. Hart, the very successful manager of the Montreal Canadians for a number of years, including 1929-30, when they won the World Championship.

Of course it is universally known that a manager cannot hope for much success unless he has his entire team ' pulling together.' The team should be welded into one happy family imbued with team spirit and *esprit de corps* ; this can be accomplished by the application of the common sense already referred to.

A manager's first concern is to see that, when his team takes the ice for its initial match of the season, it is in perfect physical condition ; grand is that *joie de vivre* feeling that accompanies perfect physical fitness. To come out of a hard game or race and to feel no effects after perhaps only a short relaxation, and with a readiness to go and do again, is, as a rule, the experience of most athletes for only a very limited number of years.

A very remarkable example of one who kept up a magnificent state of physical fitness until his sudden and unexpected end was Colonel Mayes, father of Harry Mayes, who was captain of the Grosvenor House Canadians in 1933.

Previous to their teams going on the ice for practice, managers in the States and Canada usually have their players given, for about a fortnight, various forms of gymnastic exercises that reach every muscle.

When on the ice for the first time it is as well to curb that 'run-riot' tendency that most players have which is due to their being full of energy added to the novelty of being back again on skates. Skating and 'ragging' the puck, with perhaps shooting practice, are sufficient for a while. Thus are the skating muscles hardened up and prolonged strains guarded against. Then comes the more serious practice and work-outs, with the result that after a fortnight or so on the ice a team should be in perfect training and ready to take the strain of hard play with its accompanying bumps and falls.

Should a player not be hard and fit he may feel a bump seriously which ordinarily would be merely a slight shock.

The food question, as it is for athletes in general, is a very important one for Ice-Hockey players. Here again common sense comes in without any hard-and-fast rules. Nowadays the tendency is for a man to have more what he fancies than any strict diet. Heavy sweets such as pastries are of course 'taboo,' but light ones should be permissible, especially those containing chocolate. Chocolate, like sugar, is known for its sustaining powers. The writer has found sweets extremely beneficial during the fairly long period of years that he took part in races on the water over long as well as short distances. Hard liquor is also forbidden, but beer, which seems to be universally popular with Ice-Hockey players, is allowed.

A high standard of morals must prevail during the training and playing season. There must be no getting out of condition, but care, however, must be taken to prevent players from losing weight as well as becoming stale from overwork. This is especially so over here because our season is about two months longer than the Canadian one. Percy Nicklin says that in his opinion young players do not grow stale; it is the older ones who do. The latter burn up so much energy in getting into condition that after a few games they are short of energy

On the other hand, our players are not subject to the long railway journeys of perhaps a day and a night which are often the case in Canada and the U.S.A.

Usually our teams when visiting the Continent go by air, and so the journeys are but a very few hours only.

One of the greatest assets of an Ice-Hockey club is a proper trainer. Until recent years no team in this country had one, whereas in Switzerland they were adopted long ago by some clubs. 'Sammy,' so well known to some of us 'Old Timers,' one of their first and best-known ones, was of great assistance as long ago as 1926 to the Swiss National team in the European Championship that year at Davos.

Without a proper trainer the success of a team nowadays is impossible. Sometimes it has occurred that a player has been out of a team for a week or longer with 'Charlie Horse,'[1] which is so frequent among athletes. Before a player leaves the dressing-room a good trainer will probably relieve him of pain, and with further applications next day he may be rendered absolutely fit.

Discipline amongst players must of course be maintained, in common with participants in all forms of sport.

---

[1] 'Charlie Horse' is a clot of blood which forms very deeply on the thigh or calf muscles of the leg after it has been struck a hard blow, or when these muscles have been pulled or stretched. It is different from a bruise, as the affected parts are much deeper and more painful.

It often happens that there is a trouble-maker in a club, while some athletes are less amenable to discipline than others. What seems the best way is for a manager to try and get the full confidence of all, be fair and treat them as he would wish to be treated himself. If reasonable disciplinary methods fail against a member of the team when it is necessary that they have to be applied, then for the good of the other members the best way is to get rid of him.

As the season runs on, one of the manager's most important duties is to study the tactics of the various opposing clubs. To diagnose their weak spots, bolster up his own, and devise combination plays that can be used most effectually against certain methods of offence, as well as creating defensive plays to counteract the probable successful invasion of his defending zone, are the chief essential lines to study. He must take all care that his own players understand and carry out his instructions, at the same time explaining to each one concerning his responsibility in the position in which he plays, always emphasizing the fact that co-operation and team play are the greatest factors in the success of the team.

The present game has many forms of attack and defence ; these can be shown to the players by means of a blackboard as well as on the ice. Timing of passes is the most important part of the attack, says E. P. Nicklin, also staying close to your check, the most important part of defence.

Finally, there must be a distinct understanding between the rink directorate and their team manager. The latter must be upheld in all he does and his judgment in the selection and disposition of players be accepted. If this is not recognized a lack of confidence must be indicated when no doubt there will be a mutual feeling that a change is desirable.

CHAPTER XVIII

EQUIPMENT PAST AND PRESENT IN CANADA AND HERE

In the early days of the game in Canada the equipment of players consisted of shorts and stockings, jersey, flimsy knee pads, shin guards and perhaps elbow pads. Goal-keepers were allowed to wear pads which did not give undue assistance, so for a time they either played without them or wore cricket pads. Some of the earliest teams, however, wore white trousers and not shorts. Queen's University and the Royal Military College played in them in the first recorded match, which took place on a rink in Kingston Harbour in 1887–88, about. 'The Rebels,' the Hon. Arthur Stanley's team, also wore them, as the very interesting photo shows. In this country, nearly all players wore white flannels up to the year 1914, as did those of one country on the Continent, the Belgians. The original idea in wearing flannels in preference to shorts was that the latter, with the consequent bare knees, would not be too popular with the critical Victorian audiences of our earliest hockey days! Shin pads also were worn, but underneath the flannels, so as not to mar their smart appearance. Later on, when it was found necessary to wear knee pads and elbow pads also by some, this smart appearance had to have the 'go by.' These extra means of protection had to be worn externally instead of underneath our ' all white ' kit. Light gloves, either old washing or ball-room ones, were also worn by some players. These were more for the purposes of getting a better grip of the stick and saving the hands when falling than for protection against the puck or blows from an opponent's stick. Cricket pads in lieu of shin pads for goal-keepers were adopted in London about 1908, and the natural result of trying to play against the

159

shots of the Oxford Canadians without them ! Their custodian had of course learned to use them at home, so as regards ours, it was a case of playing to learn by painful experience as well as probably learning to play !

Hockey skates were unknown to most of us except for seeing Canadians play on them. They were unobtainable in this country until perhaps the last decade. The idea in keeping to figure skates for so long was that in the narrow Princes rink most players thought it possible to turn about quicker than on hockey skates as well as get off quicker on them. This conclusion was reached, a wrong one perhaps in most cases, as the result of playing frequently against the London Canadians in 1902–03. They, however, admitted that certain of our players were remarkably quick in turning about after they had got past them.

Only in the 1910–11 season did hockey skates begin to get much used in this country. Experience on the larger rinks in Switzerland showed the necessity for adopting them. The figure skate with its two radii, probably five feet for the front four or five inches and seven feet for the remainder of the blade, did not give the necessary stability or ease of speed as did the hockey skate, which in those days was flat on the ice for its whole length.

Stability was proving a very necessary factor, because ' barging,' as we used to call it, was creeping in on the Continent.

Nowadays, however, as the game has become so speeded up, greatly increased protection has become necessary.

Every player in North America and over here is, as a rule, equipped with heavy shin and knee guards, elbow pads and stoutly padded shorts. Shoulder and arm pads are also a necessity. The last are made to afford protection to the arm below the elbow as well as above it for players who prefer this particular type. During the past season one or two players over here, however, did not wear shoulder pads. Stoutly made gauntlets, which are heavily caned back and front from the wrist upwards with flexible padded wrist, also form a very necessary part of a player's equipment.

Tube skates, it can be said, are now almost universally worn by players except goal-keepers, who use all-steel skates. The most popular type has an extra bar between the blade and the boot to stop the puck going through. Another type of goal-keeper's skate has two small upward projections from and part of the blade. These, together with the four supports to the two plates, answer the same purpose as the steel bar. The goal-keeper wears a well-padded body protector which covers him in front completely, also special protection for the shoulders and arms. His leg-pads are very substantial ; he also wears an extra heavy type of glove.

On occasions in the past, but very few in this country, some goal-keepers have worn a mask. The use of masks on the Continent, though not frequent, was more so than here.

Sticks are of three kinds : forward, defence and goal. Defence sticks are slightly larger and heavier than the forward type, while the goal stick has a specially wide blade and lower half of the handle also ; for dimensions of sticks, see rules. The taping of sticks began in this country in about 1921–22 and then only with an inferior kind of white tape, whereas in Canada it had been done for over ten years previously. The idea in taping sticks is to lengthen the life of the blade and also make shooting easier and more accurate.

Formerly sticks had a slightly curved ' Ice Lay ' but nowadays it is flat. They are made with a range of ' Lays ' ; Nos. 1 to 5 for forwards, 5 to 10 for defence players and 10 for goal-keepers, according to the importers, although one very well-known ex-defence player states that the range for defence sticks is only 5 to 7. Nos. 7 to 10 are probably ' out-sizes,' and are therefore very little in demand.

Sticks are made in two ways, one piece or laminated. The former is most popular, and is cut from Canadian Rock Elm. Of this kind some are occasionally found to have a hickory heel. The probable reason is that in making the stick the heel has not turned out too well, and so a ' false ' heel has been rendered necessary. Laminated sticks have

Rock Elm blades, Rock Elm or Ash handles with a Hickory splice at the heel.

The blades of sticks slope either to the right or left, according to the way the user shoots, or are neutral, *i.e.* upright. Neutral blades are the most popular, as players can, if they wish, easily bend them to either slope according to taste.

Finally, there remain two very important items of equipment as regards Ice-Hockey rinks : Goals and Time Clocks.

The proper kind of goal, and as now is in universal use in Canada, has the back made in two semicircles. The puck gets trapped in the net and therefore cannot rebound into play. A description of the primitive goals of former days is given in Chapter I.

Time clocks were invented by the late Herr Schlesinger of the Wiener Eislauf Verein, about seven or eight years ago. British and other teams visiting Vienna were ensured of a hearty welcome and had their interests carefully studied by the courteous inventor of an instrument without which no rink can be properly equipped.

At present the best type of time clock is installed at the Richmond rink. It has each of the three twenty-minute periods painted in distinct colours and also has two small separate clocks to time penalties.

CHAPTER XIX

JUNIOR ICE-HOCKEY

" PLAYERS must be developed in this country as every country is getting hockey-minded and will be going into it in a big way. Canada is getting short of first-class players," states E. P. Nicklin.

One extremely important result of our great success at the Olympic hockey matches last February has been to draw further and considerable attention to the great necessity of training the youth of the country in the game. As a result of the encouragement afforded by granting the necessary facilities, combined with really good coaching to boys, at Earl's Court, Richmond and Wembley, it is quite likely that we may have teams to represent us in international matches in a few years, all the members of which have learned the game in this country. Joe Smith, who has been training the boys at Earl's Court during the past season, is quite confident that some of them will be Olympic players in 1940, and no doubt Clint Benedict at Wembley and Ernest Leacock at Richmond also think the same.

In past years others besides the author have strongly advocated the training of our boys. Here is an example. As long ago as 1928, Vic Tait, who was then the popular hon. secretary to the B.I.H.A., wrote an article in the Spring number of the *British Olympic Journal* on the Olympic Ice-Hockey matches of that year. One part of his article has already been referred to in ' Olympic Hockey ' in this handbook. In another part of the article, however, he wrote, after describing the difficulties experienced in getting a team together that year, this very sound warning :—" It is quite evident that if we are going to keep pace with the standard of play in Europe, we shall have to develop the youngsters and give them better facilities. It is not clear at present how this is going to be accomplished. More rinks are the only solution (the Ice Club, Westminster and the Manchester Ice Rink were the only rinks in England then—Author), but the financial side of rink building requires answering. Undoubtedly Ice-Hockey could be made to pay its way if the public in England were given the opportunity to see first-class games, and this would enable facilities to be given to junior players to develop."

Another example was at the dinner given by the Royal Empire Society to ' The Canadas ' and combined 'Varsity teams after their match at Golders Green on February 13th, 1930. The Canadian captain, H. R. Armstrong, in the course of his speech alluded to the great importance of teaching the boys the game so that in time we should have a team home-grown and trained. This appeal, like the appeals of others, was practically unheeded for about another four years. The chief obstacles were expense and that skaters could not be deprived of any of their allotted hours. Although hockey had proved such a great success in Canada, rink managers then could not foresee any future for the game over here.

When G. S. Braden of the C.C.M. Company was over here last February, he said that if the rinks would look on junior hockey from a long-range point of view, the success of English Ice-Hockey would be assured. He also said that in Canada the success of the game can be attributed to ' Midget,' school and junior league teams. This last appeal came at a time when the ' wheels were beginning to move,' and it possibly helped give them a push. A ' big push ' is now being given to junior hockey.

The winter of 1934-35 saw R. W. Couldrey, to whom great credit is due, make a brave attempt to get school hockey going. In July 1934 he formed what was called the Public Schools Ice-Hockey Club, with Wembley as its headquarters and with the stated object of furthering the interests of the B.I.H.A. by introducing the game to the schools. The author was president of the club, F. A. de Marwicz hon. treasurer, and R. W. Couldrey hon. secretary.

Great keenness was shown by the boys during their practices at the Empire Pool and eventually a membership of about sixty was reached, with many more applications at the beginning of this last season. At the end of the 1934-35 season there was a competition between four teams for the Patton Cup. The first match was between Beaumont College and ' The Hornets ' on April 20th ; the former won 1—0. The next game was on April 23rd, between ' The Wembley Cubs,' 2, and ' The Bees,' 0, and the final, which was played immediately before a big match on April 25th, was won by ' The Cubs,' with ' Blobs ' Magwood as captain, by 2—0. It must have given the boys a bit of a thrill to play before the very large audience present that evening.

In forming the club three main principles were borne in mind :—

(1) Many boys had never seen a game of Ice-Hockey (thousands have not seen one yet). They must be encouraged to watch the senior league matches, chiefly by special reductions.

(2) Many boys had never learned to skate ; they must be encouraged to learn by special reductions.

(3) Most boys have never played Ice-Hockey in their lives. They must be coached, and that coaching should, if possible, be free.

At the beginning of last season the author wrote to F. L. Summerhayes at the Empress Stadium, Earl's Court, asking if there would be any facilities for training the youth of the country. As a result of our meeting, R. W. Couldrey was asked to arrange to call on F. Summerhayes. Owing to the latter's generosity and foresight as regards the future of the game, it was eventually arranged for the boys to play. Further, the Earl's Court management, as the result of an arrangement with the P.S.I.H.C. secretary later, was given a number of complimentary tickets to be distributed between a certain number of London Schools. Two hundred were distributed one week in December, and with each free ticket a form was given for the holder to complete if he was at all interested in the game. Fifty forms were returned completed, of which thirty were by boys between the ages of fourteen and fifteen ; of these only eight claimed to have had more than a year's experience of skating ! Anyhow, if some of them did join up, as is probable they did, there should be plenty of time in front of them to learn to skate and make good at hockey. The distribution of these tickets has therefore, no doubt, benefited the future of the game. The P.S.I.H.C. can really be said to be the parent of what is now generally described as Junior Hockey by providing a nucleus of about one hundred boys for it.

At Wembley the boys got the chance to play again in March last. Of these a number were last year's players, but so many others came along that in a short time Clint Benedict had about one hundred in hand and had to turn away many others who kept coming along. Of the hundred, forty-five were from twelve to fifteen years of age and the remainder from fifteen to twenty-four.

At Earl's Court Joe Smith is very optimistic about the boys he has been training there (*vide* his opinion early in this chapter). He is very keen on infusing team spirit and the spirit of comradeship. Next season he hopes to run a league of six teams, two of which will be called ' The London Pirates ' complete with badge of ' Skull and Cross-bones ' on their jerseys ; they will, of course, have jerseys of different colours.

At Richmond Ernest Leacock has been coaching about one hundred and forty-four boys on Sunday mornings all through the past summer ; he also claims, like Clint Benedict and Joe Smith, to have a number of very promising players.

Each of these three rinks, and it is to be hoped the new one also, will have its own league, and towards the end of the 1936-37 season a league formed from, say, the best two teams from each rink would provide a very interesting competition.

To emphasize the obvious necessity as well as other benefits to be derived from the development of junior Ice-Hockey is the fact that a number of countries on the Continent encourage it to a large extent.

To give just two examples. The very large rink in

Vienna has for a number of years had boys of graded ages playing on hockey rinks side by side and simultaneously.

Switzerland has special training for boys at Basle, Bern, Davos, St. Moritz and Zurich. It may be that in a few years the Zurich boys will develop into as formidable opponents as did the oarsmen of that town prove at Henley this last summer !

Ice-Hockey provides for youth not only a healthy sport but an education. One of the greatest benefits of the game is perhaps the development of individual ability.

Amongst the things learnt by a youngster early on in his experience as a member of his team is the value of co-operation with others in developing play, obedience to his captain and the match officials. Also the game, when played under proper conditions, in addition to great physical activity provides wholesome mental activity, the development of character and of individual initiative, also enthusiasm and self-reliance : qualities so essential for success in life in whatever work that is undertaken.

The ' goal ' of every youth should be to achieve some-thing that counts in life and ' leave footprints in the sands of time.'

To enable him to do this he must primarily build up a strong, healthy body. He should be encouraged in clean wholesome play and sports which, instead of wasting time, are building up a store of health.

CHAPTER XX

SOME INCIDENTS CONCERNING REFEREES, REFEREEING, GOAL JUDGING AND GAMES; ADVENTURES, ANECDOTES CONCERNING PLAYERS PAST AND PRESENT

' Pigs May Fly '

This was a common expression in pre-flying days. A former Ice-Hockey player, Col. J. T. C. Moore-Brabazon, M.C., M.P., took the first pig up into the air just to disprove the old saying.

THE WHISTLE, THE BELL AND THE HUNTING HORN AS REFEREE'S IMPLEMENTS

The bell replaced the whistle in Canada for very good reasons. The latter often stuck to the lips or tongue of those officiating on natural-ice rinks and prevented sometimes quick decisions being given. This trouble has also occurred on open-air ice rinks in Europe at night, and even by day occasionally at some of the higher Swiss resorts.

Another advantage the adoption of the bell over the whistle was that at times self-appointed referees among the spectators made themselves apparent ! Perhaps a dozen or so brought along whistles to use at their own discretion !

To the guide, philosopher and friend of all British hockey teams that have visited St. Moritz, Maurice Andreossi (Andy to many ' Old Timers '), the author is indebted for the story of his experience during the past winter, similar to the pre-bell days in Canada. Here it is in his words :—
" It is a well-known fact that the Italians are frantic adherents of their favourite sport. They are called ' tifosi,'

So they asked me to go to Milan to be their ' referee ' in the final for the championship of the local rivals, the Hockey Club Milan against ' Diavoli Rosso Neri.' The game had hardly started when we heard shrill whistles. Lots of people among the spectators brought along 'referee-whistles ' and at critical moments one or the other started to whistle. Thanks to the energetic intervention of the Management of the ice rink the whistling could be stopped a little but not entirely. That was a very unpleasant game and ' undecided ' too. The final had to be repeated. In a week I went to Milan again and brought along Bobby Bell [1] as second referee. The game begins and again sound the same whistles, but this time the players didn't pay any attention to that noise, because I bought two hunting-horns in a special shop for hunting-accessories and we came to an understanding before the beginning of the game with the teams. The ' tifosi ' were beaten and laughed themselves about the funny joke."

A Reason for Skating Faster !

Joe Smith overheard a player say in a dressing-room this last winter :—" Let's skate faster, boys, to get the game over quicker." This corresponds to what the driver of a sports car said when asked by a ' Speed Cop ' as to why he was exceeding the limit. " I was hurrying to get to the filling station before I ran out of petrol ! "

" Two Minutes Anyhow ! "

And now in turn here's a little refereeing story against my old friend, Maurice Andreossi, as quoted by Perley Holmes, Cambridge's captain last season, with regard to a fair body-check by Jimmy Carr in a game at St. Moritz the winter before last when the latter was captain of Cambridge. " Continental referees cause millions of queer things. About the oddest was a year ago in St. Moritz; we were leading 4—3 in the last minutes of the game.

[1] Bobby Bell was a member of the Victorias of Montreal, the first Canadian team to visit England in January 1927.

Andreossi was refereeing. The St. Moritz centre charged down the ice and ran squarely into Jimmy Carr, who didn't move an inch (he was on defence). Centre lay on ground and groaned. Andreossi said : ' Two minutes.' Jimmy said, ' Why ? That was a perfectly fair body-check.' And Andreossi replied, ' Yes, I know it was, but you take a rest for two minutes anyhow.' But we won just the same."

Kiddie Goal Judge Decisions !

Of the same match Perley Holmes relates how Cambridge ' got level ' with a goal judge. "As a matter of fact, the score should have been—no it shouldn't. In the first period we scored a goal which the goal umpire wouldn't allow, and Andreossi said we must abide by goal umpire's decision. We did. You know their habits *re* goal umpires —they have kids who don't understand English, so we can't influence them.

"Next period our right wing broke clear around the defence, skated in close and shot, hitting the post from close in. He kept on around behind the goal, saying in German ' Put it up, put it up.' The surprised kid raised his flag, and—well, we'd made up for the goal that hadn't been allowed before !"

Hockey Touring by Bus, a Useful Tip !

The Cambridge skipper said also that, " This last season the team travelled by bus ; I'll swear we pushed that bus up every hill in Europe. Don't ever do it in winter time." Good for training perhaps, all the same, probably !

Lacrosse and Golf Plus a Little Hockey on Ice !

In the Spengler Cup this year (1936) it was so warm at Davos that ice was almost non-existent. " We played," said P. H. Holmes, " our third game in a blinding wet snowstorm, on ice that had had four games played on it. Best combination of golf and lacrosse I've ever seen."

The ' Ice ' must have been exactly of the same ' quality,' as Vic Tait described it as fit for a cocktail shaker in his account of one of our matches in Olympic hockey of 1928.

A £5 WAGER

Arthur Sullivan, now Col. Arthur Sullivan, K.C., while studying Law in London in 1902–03–04, together with Donald Hingston, who was a medical student, introduced the Canadian game to us at Princes and got together the London Canadians. The latter, who is now surgeon-in-chief at the Hôtel-Dieu, a very large hospital in Montreal, was captain of the team and Arthur Sullivan was secretary. The latter is now an extremely prosperous barrister in Winnipeg, and has very sportingly given the author the details of the wager :—" The yarn you refer to about me is that, being towards the end of the month, as usual I was ' flat.' My friend, Donald, chaffingly said he would not lend me the necessary £5 which I required to go to the country for the week-end. As we strolled up Drury Lane the conversation continued. It was after midnight. Finally I suggested to Donald that I could be arrested in five minutes. The amount of the wager was the required £5. We came across a street excavation and I picked up the warning lantern that was there and proceeded to hunt for a policeman. I finally found two of them standing on a corner. I went up to them hoping they would arrest me. They didn't seem inclined to do so at first, however, so I turned around and ran. They followed and I finally thus got arrested and won my wager.

" I might add, however, that I was taken to Bow Street and was charged with drunkenness. I indignantly repudiated this suggestion and insisted that I be examined by a doctor. The doctor got me in his room, offered me a cigarette, had me walk a straight line and agreed with me that I was perfectly sober. He did ask me, however, two rather unnecessarily unkind questions. One was whether any of my ancestors had ever been confined to a lunatic asylum, and the other one was whether as a child I had ever received a severe blow on the head !

" In the morning I was remanded for one week for further inquiry, being looked upon as an American crook about whom the police desired to procure some more information. I then proceeded in the ' Black Maria ' to Brixton prison, much to the amusement of Donald. Donald offered cash bail but the police authorities would not accept it. Finally he got together two friendly householders and had me bailed out of Brixton after forty-eight hours of durance vile.

" When I appeared before Marshall, the Magistrate, he dismissed the charge against me, which was stealing a lantern, upon the very obvious ground that I had no intention of keeping the lantern. He then sent for me to see him in his private room. He was extraordinarily kind, and drew my attention to the fact that I had sat next to him at a dinner given by Lord Cave, at that time plain George Cave, of whom I was a pupil, two or three evenings before. The story got in the newspapers, I remember."

THE EXCELLENT ONE SHILLING DINNER
AND SEQUEL

This little anecdote Arthur Sullivan has said may also appear in print.

After hockey practices, a number of those of us who had been playing generally adjourned for dinner to a certain well-known grill-room in the vicinity of ' Eros.' On one occasion—note the contrast then and now !—he said : " Well, I've only a shilling left but I'm going to have a jolly good dinner." We wondered how ! In those days it was possible to get in that grill-room as much hors-d'œuvres as one wanted for ninepence ; he also had a ' Bass ' for threepence, and that is how he did the ' trick."

When Arthur Sullivan was over here just over two and a half years ago I took him to that grill-room for the sake of ' old times.' By extraordinary coincidence we were waited upon by a very ' old-time ' waiter, the only one still left there who had many a time waited on us, a merry little bunch of early-day Ice-Hockey players. Some of these were C. I (Charlie) Napier (now Major), J. J. (Jacky) and C. M. G. (Tommy) Howell, T. J. (Tom) Unite, R. A. Abercromby (Aber) (now Major), J. J. (Jack) Cawthra, and lastly but far from leastly, T. G. (Tom) Cannon, who did so much for Ice-Hockey and for so many years, as will be seen in the Officials, Past and Present, chapter.

CHAPTER XXI

SPORT AND SPORTSMANSHIP

SPORT in various forms is the recreation of the highest to the lowliest in the land, and for very many a most honourable means of livelihood ; it can do a great deal of good, and in many ways it is not only the means of making man healthier, stronger and happier, and of rendering him more equal to the fulfilment of his task in social life, but it is also one of the best means of creating friendships as well as bringing the peoples together, to establish mutual understanding and appreciation.

Sport is the one great leveller in all grades of society. So far as is known (with one exception only) the controlling bodies in all amateur sport make no distinction between competitors drawn from different social classes.

The Duke of York's camps, which he personally visits, are attended by boys of every class in life, and in these camps where they play the same games together a magnificent example is given of what great work sport can do in causing one and all to meet on an equal footing.

Britishers, all the world over, have been looked upon as the pioneers of sport. They have carried that inborn spirit of sport with them when they went to make new homes in the Dominions or elsewhere.

Our Dominions have answered us back in two of our greatest sports, cricket and Rugby football. Australia, South Africa, New Zealand, Canada and India have sent us cricket teams, and the first four countries have sent us their Rugger teams too. Some of the teams from certain of the Dominions have often more than proved our equal on occasions during exchange of visits.

Canada's love of sport, on the other hand, has, in addition to sending us teams in the two sports mentioned, introduced to us her two national games, Ice-Hockey and

Lacrosse. The first named has become a world-wide game and is spreading rapidly.

That far Japan is imbued with the spirit of sport has been shown this year by her sending representatives to take part in the Winter and in the Summer Olympic Games. In 1930 she also sent an Ice-Hockey team that vast journey across Siberia to Europe.

As a sport, Ice-Hockey, in common with certain other strenuous games, calls forth the best in man. For these sports, fleetness of foot, quickness of hand and brain, determination and fine physique, together with the ability to take heavy falls and bumps without a murmur, are some of the essential qualities.

Fair play is the ideal of sport ; without it sport loses its soul, and the spirit of chivalry is the ennobling feature of sport.

Walter Trumbull, of the *Courier*, Ontario, gave a fine definition of sport in his

Learned at the Listening Post

Sport is winning if you can,
   And keep to the sportsman's code ;
Sport is beating the other man,
   But giving him half the road ;
Being content with an even break,
   Scorning the trickster's art,
Sport is the game for the game's own sake
   And the love of a fighting heart.

The imbued spirit of sportsmanship goes further than the game, for the true sportsman carries that spirit with him in all his dealings in life.

One of the very highest qualities for a sportsman is loyalty, while self-control is the duty of every sportsman.

Some of the maxims in the sportsman's code, as set out below, formed the prelude to a booklet which gave instructions to the governing bodies of sports regarding arrangements made for their ' representative ' at the Olympic Games in Paris in July 1924. At the end of the booklet the late Lord Cadogan wrote a few words to the

British team, which began : " To play the game is the only thing in life that counts."

A sportsman,

As a player :—

Plays the game for the game's sake.

Plays for his side and not for himself.

Is a good loser as well as winner, *i.e.* is generous in defeat and modest in victory.

Accepts the umpire's decisions absolutely and never interferes or tries to argue with him.

Is unselfish and always ready to help others become proficient.

Carries out his captain's or his coach's orders without question or criticism.

Would rather lose than win by unfair means.

As a spectator :—

Is impartial by applauding the good play of both sides.

Does not ' boo ' the referee when he gives a decision with which you do not agree.

Does not want his side to win if it does not deserve to do so.

The test of true sportsmanship is not the ability with which something is done but the spirit in which it is done.

Near the title-page of a handbook on one of our very greatest of games, some little while ago appeared the famous lines which Colonel Ronald Campbell, during his reign at the Aldershot Gymnasium, caused to be boldly displayed for the benefit of young soldiers :—

> " For when the one Great Scorer
> Comes to write against your name,
> He writes not that you won or lost
> But how you ' played the game '."

Ice Hockey Officials Past & Present
JF Ahearne, Col AA Sullivan KC, TG Cannon, JCP Magwood, Maj BM Patton, Sq Ldr VH Tait, PV Hunter CBE

British Ice Hockey Champions Up to 2020

Compiled in September 2020 by Paul Breeze (editor, www.icehockeyreview.co.uk) from a variety of sources, including:

https://www.hockeyarchives.info/archives.htm
https://internationalhockey.fandom.com/wiki/Early_British_champions
Harris, Martin C: "Homes of British Ice Hockey" (Tempus 2005)
Patton, Major BM: "Ice Hockey" (Routledge: London, 1936)
Roberts, Stewart (ed): "Ice Hockey Annual" (various years)

Niagara Challenge Cup

1897: The first organised indoor competition using special ice hockey rules was organised at the Niagara rink in London.

The "Virginia Water bandy team" beat Camberley 2-0 in the final to win the New Niagara Challenge Cup

1898: Niagara IHC beat Virginia Water 17-5 over two games on 7th and 8th Jan 1898 to win the Challenge Cup

In what appears to have been a separate competition played later in the year,

1898: Niagara IHC – beat Princes 2-1 in the semi final (OT) on 16th March and then Niagara II in the final 4-0 on 2nd April 1898. This was the first time that the term "English Champions" was accorded.

1898-99: Niagara IHC - beat Princes 5-1 to win the last Niagara Challenge Cup (16th March 1899), however Patton (1936) lists Princes Club as English champions for that period.

English Club Championship

1899: Princes Ice Hockey Club - after winning challenge matches over other teams (per Patton, 1936)

1900: Princes Ice Hockey Club – after winning challenge matches over other teams (per Patton, 1936)

1901: Princes Ice Hockey Club – beat Oxford University 21-11 over two games (6th Feb & 6th Mar 1901)

1902: Cambridge University – beat Princes club 9-5 (15th Mar1902)

1903: London Canadians - beat Princes Club 8-4 (OT)

English Ice Hockey League 1903-04

1904: London Canadians
A 5-team league competition – the first ever to be held in Europe
Final Positions: 1 London Canadians 14pts, 2 Prince's Club 12pts, 3 Argyll 8pts, 4 Amateur Skating Club 6pts, 4 Cambridge University 2.

English Club Championship

1905: Princes Ice Hockey Club – no opposition teams to play

1906: Princes Ice Hockey Club – beat Oxford Canadians 11-8 over two legs (20th & 21st March 1906)

1907: Oxford Canadians – beat Princes 3-2 (16th March 1907)

1908: Princes Ice Hockey Club beat Oxford Canadians 7-2- (17th March 1908)

1909: Princes Ice Hockey Club - unchallenged

1910: Oxford Canadians – beat Princes 17-3 over two games

1911: Oxford Canadians – beat Princes 11-2 18th Feb

1912: Princes Ice Hockey Club - unchallenged

1913: Oxford Canadians -

1914: Princes Ice Hockey Club – beat Oxford Canadians (21st Apr 1914)

1915-1927: no championship titles awarded

No official league competitions due to World War 1 and lack of ice rinks in its aftermath

1928: United Services - after a series of challenge games

1929: United Services - United Services won the Southern Section and beat Manchester 5-6 (6th April 1929) @ Manchester for the "English Club Championship":

1930: London Lions beat Glasgow in a play off for the first ever "British Championship".

Semi Finals: London Lions beat United Services. Princes beat Cambridge University 3-0 at Park Lane Ice Rink (30th April). London Lions beat Princes in the southern final on 1st & 2nd May at to reach the overall final.

Northern Championship: The Glasgow team was assembled utilising a pool of players from the various Scottish League teams. Glasgow beat Manchester over two legs 1:1 and 3:2 to qualify for the national final.

The final was played on 17th May 1930 at Golders Green Ice Rink, at the time the home of the London Lions. The Lions beat Glasgow 2-1. The teams competed for the "Patton Cup" which was awarded for the one and only time.

English Club Championship (cont'd...)

1931: London Lions – unbeaten in challenges against other teams

English & Scottish League Period

Season	English League	Scottish National League
1929-30	Cambridge University	Glasgow Mohawks
1930-31		Kelvingrove
1931-32	Oxford University	
1932-33	Oxford University	Bridge of Weir
1933-34	Grosvenor house Canadians	Kelvingrove
1934-35	Streatham	Bridge of Weir
	English National League	
1935-36	Wembley Lions	Glasgow Mohawks
1936-37	Wembley Lions	Glasgow Mohawks
1937-38	Harringay Racers	Perth Panthers
1938-39	Harringay Greyhounds	Dundee Tigers
1939-40	Harringay Greyhounds	Dundee Tigers
1940-46	*No official league competitions due to World War 2*	
1946-47	Brighton Tigers	Perth Panthers
1947-48	Brighton Tigers	East - Dundee Tigers / West Paisley Pirates
1948-49	Harringay Racers	Fife Flyers
1949-50	Streatham	Fife Flyers
1950-51	Nottingham Panthers	Paisley Pirates
1951-52	Wembley Lions	Ayr Raiders
1952-53	Streatham	Ayr Raiders
1953-54	Nottingham Panthers	Paisley Pirates

British League Period (BL)

Season	British League Champions
1954–55	Harringay Racers
1955–56	Nottingham Panthers
1956–57	Wembley Lions
1957–58	Brighton Tigers
1958–59	Paisley Pirates
1959–60	Streatham

Note: 1960 only – end of season play off for the British Championship won by Brighton Tigers, who beat Nottinham Panthers 6-5 over two legs (3-2 and 3-3)

Icy Smith Cup Period

From 1966, the Icy Smith Cup was played as knockout cup competition between teams from the Northern and Southern leagues. From 1976, the qinners were acknowledged as British Champions and the previous winners were retrospectively also accorded that title.

Season	Ice Smith Cup Winners	Northern League Champions	Southern League Champions
1965-66	Murrayfield Racers		
1966-67	Glasgow Dynamos	Paisley Mohawks	
1967-68	Paisley Mohawks	Paisley Mohawks	
1968-69	Murrayfield Racers	Paisley Mohawks	
1969-70	Murrayfield Racers	Murrayfield Racers	
1970-71	Murrayfield Racers	Murrayfield Racers	Sussex Senators
1971-72	Murrayfield Racers	Murrayfield Racers	Sussex Senators
1972-73	Whitley Warriors	Dundee Rockets	Altrincham Aces
1973-74	Whitley Warriors	Whitley Bay Warriors	Streatham Redskins
1974-75	Murrayfield Racers	Whitley Bay Warriors	Streatham Redskins
1975-76	Ayr Bruins	Murrayfield Racers	Streatham Redskins
1976-77	Fife Flyers	Fife Flyers	Streatham Redskins
1977-78	Fife Flyers	Fife Flyers	Solihull Barons
1978-79	Murrayfield Racers	Murrayfield Racers	Streatham Redskins
1979-80	Murrayfield Racers	Murrayfield Racers	London Phoenix Flyers
1980-81	Murrayfield Racers	Murrayfield Racers	Streatham Redskins
1981-82	Dundee Rockets (Mecca Leisure Trophy)	Dundee Rockets	Streatham Redskins
			ENL 81-82 Streatham

Notes: From 1978/79 Southern League became known as the Inter City League (ICL)
The Southern League had a separate Midland Division from 75/76 onwards. and this became known as the English League North for seasons 78/79 to 81/82.
Season 1981/82 - English National League played as a separate competition for one season only

The first ever British Championship Play Off weekend was held at Streatham Ice Rink in April 1982 and saw Dundee Rockets beat Blackpool Seagulls 16-4 in the first semi-final and Streaham Redskins beat Murrayfield Racers 9-5 in the second. The Mecca Leisure Trophy was sponsored by rink owners Mecca and the teams' travel and hotel costs were sponsored by Top Brass Lager. Highlights of the games were filmed and shown by Thames Television.

British League Period (HBL)

Season	British League Division 1 League Champions	Play Off Winners British Championship
1982–83	Dundee Rockets	Dundee Rockets
		(Heineken Trophy – played at Streatham)

	Heineken League Premier Division Champions	Heineken Championship (at Wembley Arena)
1983–84	Dundee Rockets	Dundee Rockets
1984–85	Durham Wasps	Fife Flyers
1985–86	Durham Wasps	Murrayfield Racers
1986–87	Murrayfield Racers	Durham Wasps
1987–88	Murrayfield Racers	Durham Wasps
1988–89	Durham Wasps	Nottingham Panthers
1989–90	Cardiff Devils	Cardiff Devils
1990–91	Durham Wasps	Durham Wasps
1991–92	Durham Wasps	Durham Wasps
1992–93	Cardiff Devils	Cardiff Devils
1993–94	Cardiff Devils	Cardiff Devils
1994–95	Sheffield Steelers	Sheffield Steelers
1995–96	Sheffield Steelers	Sheffield Steelers

Notes: In 1982 a new British League was formed from the top teams in the previous Northern and Southern leagues. It was played in Divisions 1, 2 and 3 for one season and then under the sponsorship of Heineken became the Heineken League from 1983 with Premier Division, and Division 1 and an unsponsored Division 2. The end of season Heineken Championship Play Offs at Wembley Arena represented the British Championship.

Superleague Period (ISL)

Season	ISL League Champions	ISL Play Offs
1996–97	Cardiff Devils	Sheffield Steelers
1997–98	Ayr Scottish Eagles	Ayr Scottish Eagles
1998–99	Manchester Storm	Cardiff Devils
1999–2000	Bracknell Bees	London Knights
2000–01	Sheffield Steelers	Sheffield Steelers
2001–02	Belfast Giants	Sheffield Steelers
2002–03	Sheffield Steelers	Belfast Giants

Elite League Period (EIHL)

Season	EIHL League Champions	British Championship (EIHL Play Offs)
2003/04	Sheffield Steelers	Sheffield Steelers
2004/05	Coventry Blaze	Coventry Blaze
2005/06	Belfast Giants	Newcastle Vipers
2006/07	Coventry Blaze	Nottingham Panthers
2007/08	Coventry Blaze	Sheffield Steelers
2008/09	Sheffield Steelers	Sheffield Steelers
2009/10	Coventry Blaze	Belfast Giants
2010/11	Sheffield Steelers	Nottingham Panthers
2011/12	Belfast Giants	Nottingham Panthers

Season	EIHL League Champions	Erhardt Conference	Gardiner Conference	Patton Conference	EIHL Play Offs
2012/13	Nottingham Panthers	Belfast Giants	Braehead Clan		Nottingham Panthers
2013/14	Belfast Giants	Belfast Giants	Dundee Stars		Sheffield Steelers
2014/15	Sheffield Steelers	Nottingham Panthers	Braehead Clan		Coventry Blaze
2015/16	Sheffield Steelers	Cardiff Devils	Braehead Clan		Nottingham Panthers
2016/17	Cardiff Devils	Cardiff Devils	Braehead Clan		Sheffield Steelers
2017/18	Cardiff Devils	Cardiff Devils	Fife Flyers	Manchester Storm	Cardiff Devils
2018/19	Belfast Giants	Belfast Giants	Braehead Clan	Guildford Flames	Cardiff Devils

2019/20 – EIHL season incomplete due to coronavirus pandemic – no championship titles awarded.

Brighton Tigers
A Story Of Sporting Passion

By Kevin Wilsher & Stewart Roberts
Published April 2020
ISBN: 978-1-527255-63-0

A lot of modern ice hockey fans probably won't know that the Brighton Tigers were a big part of hockey history from the opening of their superb SS (Sports Stadium) in the 1930s right up until it was controversially closed in 1965 just when British ice hockey was slowly edging towards its next golden era.

While the main thrust of this book is, obviously, the Tigers teams of the 1930s to the 1960s there is a very interesting introduction that tells of earlier rinks in the Brighton area – namely the Victorian circular rink that operated from 1897-1901 and then a more modern facility at Hove (1929-1932).

This book is an absolute mine of information. Who knew, for example, that while most leisure facilities were closed for the duration of World War 2, the Brighton Sports Stadium had ice hockey matches on every week featuring a mixture of local players and visiting Canadian servicemen...?

There is a complete player directory of everybody who ever turned out for the Tigers teams - and that is quite an achievement in itself bearing in mind the scarcity of statistical information from the pre-war and immediate post war periods - as well as lots of great photos of many of the stars.

I may be slightly biased as this is the sort of book that I like to produce myself - as well as to read - but it means that I can easily appreciate the huge amount of work that is involved in putting this sort of thing together – seeking out all the facts and figures, getting permission for all the photos, checking and rechecking all the data...

Whether you're a modern hockey fan – or a bit of a nostalgia fan like me – or maybe know nothing about it and want to find out more, this book is definitely worth read.

Reviewed by Paul Breeze, Editor of Ice Hockey Review

S & T SALES & MARKETING LTD
www.sandtsales.co.uk

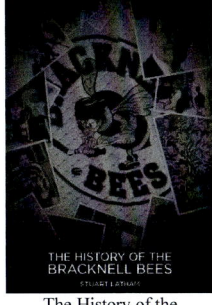

The History of the Swindon
Wildcats 1986 – 2016
ISBN No: 978-0-9530608-7-0
A4 Size - £22.99

The History of the
Bracknell Bees
ISBN No 978-0-9530608-8-7
A4 Size - £24.99

The History of Ice Hockey in
Peterborough
ISBN No: 978-0-9530608-6-3
A4 Size - £19.99

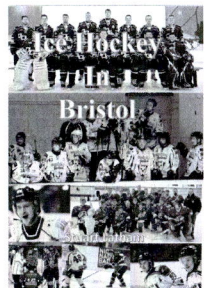

60 Years of the
Altrincham Aces
ISBN No: 978-1-8381165-0-7
B5 Size - 176 pages - £15.99

The Deeside Dragons
ISBN No: 978-1-8381165-3-8
204 pages B5 Size - £15.99

Ice Hockey in Bristol
ISBN No: 978-1-8381165-2-1
B5 Size

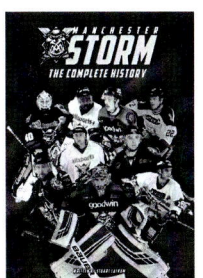

The Rise and Fall of the
Manchester Phoenix
ISBN No: 978-1-8381165-6-9
B5 Size

Manchester Storm
The Complete History
ISBN No: 978-1-8381165-4-5
B5 Size

S&T SALES AND
MARKETING Ltd

**Book Publishing and
Engineering Consultants**

For enquiries:

+44 7702035951

stuartlatham@sandtsales.co.uk

www.sanadtsales.co.uk

185

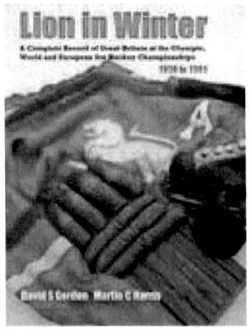

Lion in Winter: A Complete Record of Great
Britain at the Olympic, World and European Ice
Hockey Championships 1910 - 1981
By David S Gordon & Martin C Harris
Publication Date: 22/09/2019
ISBN: 9781527247475

Lion in Winter is the gripping tale of the Great
Britain ice hockey team's fluctuating fortunes,
from being the first European Champions in 1910
through to the nadir 0f 1981, when a drop to the
bottom of the world rankings resulted in a self-
imposed exile from international competition.
Detailing the pinnacle of international achievement with victory at the 1936
Winter Olympics, it chronicles a roller-coaster record from underdogs to
bulldogs - and back again - several times. No other champion ice hockey
nation has scaled the heights and plumbed the depths like the British.

A definitive work of record, it is researched and written by two of the game's
foremost historians and features the only complete GB Player register ever
published, complemented by a wide variety of rare illustrations.

ICE COLD MURDER –
an ice hockey murder mystery
By Michael A Chambers
Publication Date: September 2017
ISBN: 978-0953939831

The town of Merrivale is of average size and
population that contains the usual housing
and amenities it warrants, and Saturday
afternoons are strictly reserved for the weekly
game of football, hockey and rugby as well as a
shopping spree for the locals.

When a body is found within hockey owner Mark Atkin's establishment,
Inspector Dilley has to unravel this terrible scene in order to find out what
happened. Amongst a complexity of doors, keys and camera pictures which
have much to do with it all.

Many people have much to do with the events that occur this day which puts
them 'in the frame' within this much troubled club.

Who did it?

Copies available from the author. Contact Michael via e-mail at:
spikc2004@yahoo.co.uk

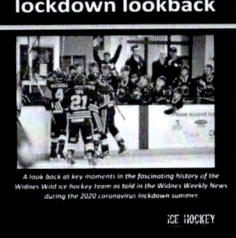
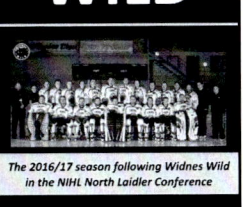

ALSO AVAILABLE FROM THE SAME PUBLISHER

Interesting Books...
...Fascinating Subjects!

www.poshupnorth.com

Guns & Pencils
ISBN 978-0-953978-22-9

purple patches

a collection of poems, songs and short stories from the fountain pen of lucy london

Purple Patches
ISBN: 978-1909643-00-0

WILFRED OWEN: CENTENARY

Wilfed Owen: Centenary
ISBN: 978-1-909643-36-9

FEMALE POETS OF THE FIRST WORLD WAR

VOLUME ONE

COMPILED BY LUCY LONDON

Female Poets - Vol 1
ISBN 9781909643-02-4
126 pages paperback

Female Poets - Vol 2
ISBN 978-1-909643-17-8
186 pages paperback

No Woman's Land
ISBN 978-1-909643-07-9
128 pages paperback

AVIATOR POETS & WRITERS OF WW1

Aviator Poets & Writers
ISBN: 978-1-909643-22-2

POETS, WRITERS & ARTISTS ON THE SOMME 1916

The Somme 1916
ISBN 9781909643-24-6
136 pages paperback
with b/w photographs

ARRAS, MESSINES, PASSCHENDAELE & MORE
POETS, WRITERS, ARTISTS & NURSES IN 1917

Arras, Messines, Passchendaele & More
ISBN: 978-1-909643-21-5 -
150 Pages Paperback
]

Women Casualties Of The Great War In Military Cemeteries

Volume 1: Belgium & France

**Women Casualties – Vol1
Belgium & France**
ISBN 978-1-909643-26-0
86 pages paperback

POETS' CORNERS IN FOREIGN FIELDS

Poets' Corners In Foreign Fields
ISBN 978-1-909643-08-6
72 pages paperback

Darwen Football Club
ISBN: 978-0953978-24-3

BLACKPOOL TO BOND STREET

The Fascinating Story of Amy Blackburn Pioneer Of The Makeover.
By Jean Shaw
Edited by Paul Breeze & Lucy London

Blackpool to Bond Street
ISBN: 978-0953978-25-0

Colne Giants
by Paul Breeze & Stuart Greenfield

Tales From The Forgotten World of Knur and Spell
With a foreword by Geoff Cramble

Colne Giants
ISBN: 978-953978-23-6

By mail order from *www.poshupnorth.com*, Amazon, Kindle, WW1 Publishing and many other quality outlets...!